DISASTERS

Scholastic Inc.

GIANT ROCKFALL IN HUNZA VALLEY, NORTHEAST PAKISTAN, JANUARY 2010

CONTENTS

DISASTROUS WEATHER

A Deadly Year 8	Tornado Facts 16	Big Freeze 24
Weather Machine 10	Hurricanes 18	Avalanche! 26
Tornadoes 12	Hurricane Katrina 20	Wildfires 28
Storm Chasers 14	Lightning Strikes 22	

UNSTABLE EARTH

Landslides 32	All in Ruins 40	Lava and Lahars 48
Restless Earth 34	Aftermath of an Earthquake 42	Volcano Facts 50
Earth Scientists 36	Living with Earthquakes 44	
Earthquakes 38	Stratovolcanoes 46	

TROUBLED WATER

Flooding 54	Tsunamis 58
Monsoon Floods 56	Tsunami Timeline 60

HOW PEOPLE CAUSE DISASTERS

Causing Disaster 64	Future Disaster 70	Pandemics 76
Thirsty Work 66	Tackling Global Warming 72	Malaria 78
Global Warming 68	Overburdened Earth 74	

THE THREAT FROM SPACE

Asteroid Impact 82	The Final Disaster 86	Glossary 88
Solar Storms 84		Index 91
		Credits 93

DISASTROUS WEATHER

FIND OUT

?

HOW do tornadoes form?
WHAT is the most deadly type of lightning?
WHICH hurricane devastated a whole city?

A DEADLY YEAR

A natural disaster strikes at least once a month somewhere around the world. In 2023, disasters included cyclones, wildfires, floods, and deadly earthquakes.

DROUGHT: SPAIN, APRIL—6 MILLION+ AFFECTED

WILDFIRES: HAWAII, AUGUST—102 KILLED

HURRICANE OTIS: MEXICO, OCTOBER—45+ KILLED

Marrakesh-Safi earthquake
On September 8, a magnitude 6.9 earthquake shook Morocco, killing almost 3,000 people.

Brazil landslides
In February, flash floods caused devastating landslides in São Paulo, Brazil.

STORM DANIEL: MEDITERRANEAN

September saw the deadliest storm in 10 years hit the Mediterranean. In Greece, six months' worth of rain fell in just 24 hours. Storm Daniel then reached the coast of Libya, Africa, causing dangerous flooding. Two dams burst and more than 5,000 people died.

City collapse
The port city of Derna, Libya, was left in ruins after the floods brought by Storm Daniel.

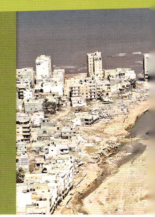

An estimated

86,000 PEOPLE DIED

in natural disasters in 2023.

CYCLONE MOCHA: MYANMAR AND BANGLADESH, MAY—145 KILLED

EARTHQUAKES: TURKEY AND SYRIA, FEBRUARY—55,000+ KILLED

FLOODS: BANGLADESH, INDIA, PAKISTAN, AND NEPAL, JUNE–AUGUST—600+ KILLED

Extreme cold
China reported a record low temperature of −63°F (−53°C) in January.

EUROPE — SPAIN, GREECE, LIBYA, TURKEY AND SYRIA
AFRICA — MADAGASCAR, MOZAMBIQUE, AND MALAWI
ASIA — CHINA; MYANMAR, BANGLADESH, INDIA, PAKISTAN, AND NEPAL; INDONESIA
AUSTRALIA

Tropical Cyclone Freddy
This fierce storm lasted five weeks in the southern Indian Ocean, flooding Madagascar, Mozambique, and Malawi.

Mount Merapi eruption
This Indonesian volcano erupted on December 3, killing 22 hikers.

WILDFIRES: CANADA

Throughout the summer, record-breaking wildfires in Canada burned an area about the size of Florida. The smoke from these fires drifted south, polluting the air across the eastern United States.

Orange skies
Smoke from the Canadian wildfires turned the New York skyline a hazy orange for two days in June 2023.

WEATHER MACHINE

Weather is the state of the atmosphere anywhere above Earth. In some places, it stays calm and settled for months. In others, it switches between calm and stormy, with dangerous extremes of rain, drought, heat, and cold.

RESTLESS AIR

This satellite image of Earth shows swirling clouds moving through the atmosphere. Clouds are a visible part of our planet's weather machine—a complex cycle of air and water set in motion by the Sun.

SUN POWER

The Sun's energy warms land, water, and air at different rates. Clouds form when warmed air rises. As it cools, it condenses into billions of tiny water droplets or ice crystals, which float in the air.

Polar jet stream
This narrow band of cold, fast-moving air can trigger extreme weather, such as snowstorms and floods, when it shifts.

Heat energy from the Sun

50 miles (85 km):
the height of the Earth's highest clouds

Weather front
Long rows of clouds show where different air masses meet. This meeting place is called a weather front. Weather fronts often result in changeable weather, such as rain or snow, across a whole region.

Hurricane Beryl, 2024
Huge storms like Hurricane Beryl are generated by heat stored in the oceans, which rises to form moisture-filled clouds. Strong winds set the clouds spinning, often forming giant spirals.

Cloudy skies
Different clouds form depending on the altitude warm air rises to, and its temperature. Streams of converging air, forced to rise when they meet, cause cumulus clouds and showers. Strong, rapidly cooling updrafts can create thunderclouds.

ATMOSPHERE

Scientists divide the atmosphere into five layers. Each layer gets less dense, or thinner, the farther you travel from Earth's surface, because there is less air pressing down from above.

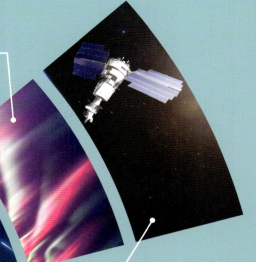

Thermosphere:
50–440 miles (80–700 km)
Lights called auroras flicker in this layer of the upper atmosphere.

Stratosphere:
7.5–31 miles (12–50 km)
This layer contains some high-level, icy clouds.

Exosphere:
440–6,200 miles (700–10,000 km)
Satellites orbit Earth in this layer. From here, the air's gas molecules and atoms escape into space.

Mesosphere:
31–55 miles (50–88.5 km)
Meteors burn up in this layer, leaving fiery trails in the sky.

Troposphere:
0–7.5 miles (0–12 km)
This is the layer we live in, where our weather occurs.

Doldrums
This band of hot, humid air stretching around the Equator is the site of frequent thunderstorms.

THE WEATHER LAYER

Weather happens in the troposphere, the layer of air just above Earth's surface. This layer contains nearly all of the atmosphere's water, and most of its clouds.

Midlatitude storm

Weather front

Midlatitude storm damage
Midlatitude storms start where a mass of cold polar air meets warmer air from the middle latitudes north and south of the Equator, forming storm clouds. This type of storm occurs in both the Northern and Southern Hemispheres.

Thunderstorm
Floods and landslides may occur when thunderstorms bring torrential rain. These local storms form when warm, moist air rises rapidly over land or sea, building into huge, towering thunderclouds.

TORNADOES

Reaching down from stormy skies, tornadoes are short-lived but unleash some of the fastest winds on Earth, often leaving a trail of devastation.

INSIDE A TORNADO

A tornado contains a low-pressure core surrounded by a condensation funnel. Air rushes in and spins around the funnel, while a powerful downdraft sucks air through the funnel toward the ground.

Danger zone
Extreme tornadoes can have wind speeds of up to 321 mph (516.6 kph) and be up to 2.6 miles (4.2 km) wide.

LIFE OF A TORNADO

Tornadoes are formed beneath supercells, or rotating thunderstorms, when a funnel drops from a cloud and makes contact with the ground. Most tornadoes last 10–15 minutes. Rare, powerful ones may last for about an hour.

1 Funnel forming
A funnel of air reaches down from a cloud at the base of a rotating supercell. The funnel gains speed as it spins.

2 Touching the ground
The funnel lengthens until it reaches the ground. Dust and debris stirred up by the wind form a sleeve around the core.

Every year, around 1,200 TORNADOES hit the United States.

Tornado aftermath
Joplin, Missouri, lies in ruins after an EF5 tornado swept through the town, leaving a path of destruction 1 mile (1.6 km) wide and killing 158 people.

Disastrous Weather

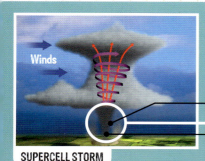
SUPERCELL STORM — Winds, Condensation funnel, Core

CLOSE-UP OF CONDENSATION FUNNEL — Updraft, Downdraft, Spiraling winds, Debris

3
...ring
...ng winds at the base scour ...ound. The tornado is now ...maximum strength.

4
Shrinking and slowing
Although still powerful, the tornado's wind speeds start to drop. As the tornado weakens, it starts to tilt and lose its shape.

5
Fading away
The tilt increases, heavy debris drops to the ground, and the tornado fades away. This stage normally lasts for only a few minutes.

EYEWITNESS

NAME: Dr. Kevin Kikta
DATE: May 22, 2011
LOCATION: Joplin, MO, USA
DETAILS: Dr. Kikta was an emergency room doctor on duty at St. John's Regional Medical Center in Joplin on the day the tornado struck.

> We heard a loud horrifying sound like a large locomotive ripping through the hospital. We heard glass shattering. . . . walls collapsing, people screaming, the ceiling caving in above us. . . . The whole process took about 45 seconds, but seemed like eternity.

DANGER SIGNS

Tornadoes can develop quickly. The first warning for people in tornado-prone areas often comes from radio, TV, or a smartphone alert that includes sound and vibration. On average, people have only 10–15 minutes to find shelter after hearing a warning.

Tornado Warning Signs
- Dark, often greenish sky
- Large hail
- A massive, dark, low-lying cloud (particularly if rotating)
- A loud roar, similar to a freight train's roar

Shelter
Underground shelters provide some protection from winds and flying debris.

Giant Hailstones
Hailstones the size of tennis balls, each weighing up to 2.2 pounds (1 kg), can be an extra hazard during some storms.

STORM CHASERS

In 2009 and 2010, "storm chaser" Sean Casey crisscrossed the US Midwest in the ultimate tornado-proof machine. Called the Tornado Intercept Vehicle (TIV), it protected a team of scientists involved in the VORTEX2 project—a mission to discover how and why tornadoes form. By collecting more information about these deadly storms, scientists hope to increase warning times and therefore save lives.

On June 5, 2009, the VORTEX2 team made history when they intercepted a tornado and filmed its entire life cycle.

11:30 AM	The team drove to Wyoming, where supercell storms were forecast for that day.
2:00 PM	They headed to a supercell located in Goshen County.
3:00 PM	The team set up Doppler radar equipment to scan the storm.
3:37 PM	A tornado warning was issued.
4:07 PM	The tornado touched down near LaGrange, Wyoming.
4:10 PM	The team experienced softball-sized hail.
4:31 PM	The tornado faded away, and the warning was lifted.

EYEWITNESS

" Driving into the heart of a tornado was both exhilarating and scary. Inside that howling, sand-blasting wind, the whole vehicle was shaking. After the initial impact, once I knew we would be all right, I was able to relax enough to enjoy the moment. "

Sean Casey

Tornado Intercept Vehicle (TIV)

The TIV has drop-down panels to prevent strong winds from blowing underneath it, and hydraulic spikes that anchor it to the ground.

- Bulletproof glass
- Filming turret
- Instrument mast
- Antiwind flap
- Ground spike
- Armored side panel

TORNADO FACTS

Tornadoes strike in every continent except Antarctica. The United States tops the danger list, followed by Canada, Brazil, and Bangladesh. Tornadoes often hit cities and towns, causing massive damage.

TORNADO SCALE

The Enhanced Fujita (EF) scale rates tornado strength based on estimated wind speed and damage caused. EF0 tornadoes damage signs and break off small branches. EF5 tornadoes can flatten buildings.

Wind speeds and damage

EF0:	65–85 mph (105–137 kph)	MINOR DAMAGE
EF1:	86–110 mph (138–177 kph)	MODERATE DAMAGE
EF2:	111–135 mph (178–217 kph)	CONSIDERABLE DAMAGE
EF3:	136–165 mph (218–266 kph)	SEVERE DAMAGE
EF4:	166–200 mph (267–322 kph)	DEVASTATING DAMAGE
EF5:	200+ mph (322+ kph)	TOTAL DEVASTATION

BLOWN AWAY

People have reported seeing all sorts of things being picked up and carried by twisters. These range from lightweight paper to animals, cars, and trailers.

Pressure drop

Air pressure inside a tornado's funnel can be 10 percent lower than the air pressure outside. Low pressure and powerful winds allow tornadoes to shift heavy objects, such as cars.

Whirling record

Teenager Matt Suter holds the record for the longest distance a person has been blown along by a tornado. He was carried 1,307 feet (398 m)—and he survived!

302 mph (486 kph): the **FASTEST** wind speed measured in a TORNADO

TORNADO ALLEY

The Midwestern US states are famous for tornadoes, with around 300–400 striking every year. Nicknamed "Tornado Alley," this region consists of flat, open plains where cold and warm air fronts often meet, creating the perfect mix for violent supercell thunderstorms.

Between 1993 and 2022, Texas had more tornadoes than any other state, with an average of 136 a year. Tornadoes are also common in the Gulf Coast states, including Alabama and Florida.

Oklahoma City, Oklahoma, in the heart of Tornado Alley, has been hit by over 175 tornadoes since 1890. In 1974, 2013, and 2018 it was struck by 5 twisters in a single day.

PEAK TIMES

In the United States, tornadoes occur throughout the year, but they are most common on warm afternoons in spring and early summer. From 1998 to 2022, May and June were the top two months on average for the number of tornadoes in the US.

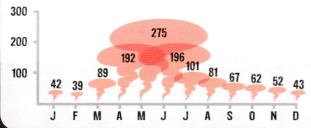

Tornadoes have an average height of **328–980** (100–300 m) **feet**, depending on climate conditions.

Traveling at an average speed of **28 mph**, (45 kph) a tornado can outpace an Olympic sprinter.

695: the number of people killed in the tri-state tornado outbreak in 1925, which struck Missouri, Illinois, and Indiana

HIT AND MISS

Although large tornadoes can kill hundreds of people, every year there are lucky escapes. In April 2012, a swarm of tornadoes struck Texas, but not one person died. The tornadoes hit during the day, and many people were able to reach shelter in time.

Tragic figures
Bangladesh holds the record for the most deaths in a single tornado strike.

1,300: the number of people killed in Bangladesh by a single tornado in 1989

HURRICANES

Hurricanes and typhoons are tropical cyclones, the world's most violent storms. Most form in late summer over warm, sun-drenched seas. Their winds can gust over 157 miles per hour (253 kph), causing colossal damage if they drift over land.

MEASURING HURRICANES

The Saffir-Simpson scale measures the strengths of tropical cyclones, including hurricanes and typhoons. Category 1 cyclones cause little damage. Category 5 storms can tear off roofs and flood buildings far inland.

HOW HURRICANES FORM

Hurricanes form when the ocean's temperature is at least 80.5°F (27°C). Surface winds suck up moisture from the sea, creating bands of thunderclouds.

Spreading out
Cool, dry air flows outward from the center, sucking up more air from below.

Eye wall
This inner ring of thunderstorms can drop 10 inches (25 cm) of rain in a single hour.

Wind direction
Winds blow counterclockwise in the Northern Hemisphere and clockwise in the Southern Hemisphere.

9 DAYS: the LIFESPAN of a typical HURRICANE

Tropical depression and storm
A tropical depression over the sea grew into a tropical storm, with wind speeds of more than 39 mph (63 kph).

Category 1 hurricane
The storm became a Cat hurricane when its winds over 74 mph (119 kph).

LIFE OF A HURRICANE

These satellite images show Hurricane Katrina, which battered New Orleans in 2005. The pictures are color coded to indicate the sea's surface temperature: red and orange are warmest, while blue is cold.

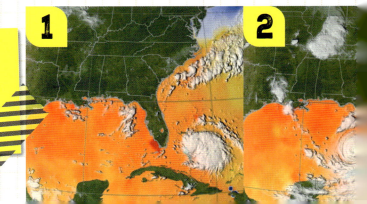

Disastrous Weather

AN INSIDE VIEW

If you could slice through a hurricane, you would see walls of clouds spiraling around its calm central eye. The spiral is made up of giant bands of rain; it rotates because Earth rotates.

Giant stretch
The largest tropical cyclones can have a diameter of up to 675 miles (1,086 km).

Reaching the top
The top of a tropical cyclone can tower 8 miles (13 km) above the sea's surface.

Eye of the storm
The eye is a calm, warm area at the storm's center.

Rain bands
Warm, moist air rises and creates bands of thunderclouds, separated by zones of clearer air.

Spiraling winds
Powerful winds spiral around the eye, sucking up water vapor from the sea.

Suction effect
Low air pressure in the eye raises the sea level below, creating a storm surge if the hurricane drifts over land.

Low pressure
Air pressure in the eye is lower than elsewhere in the storm.

Category 3 hurricane
The hurricane intensified to Category 3, sucking up moisture while crossing the Gulf of Mexico.

Maximum-strength hurricane
Katrina briefly became a Category 5 hurricane before it drifted over land. Here, the eye is clearly visible at the center of the spiral.

Tropical storm and depression
The hurricane weakened into a tropical storm, then into a depression, as it tracked northward across the United States.

19

HURRICANE KATRINA

In 2005, Hurricane Katrina struck the Gulf Coast of the United States. The storm caused chaos in New Orleans, Louisiana, as floodwaters surged through the streets, killing more than 1,800 people and leaving thousands homeless.

AUG. 23
Tropical depression
The National Hurricane Center in Florida issued a weather warning about a tropical depression forming over the Bahamas.

TROPICAL DEPRESSION TRACKING WEST

AUG. 25 (6:30 PM)
Florida
The hurricane struck the tip of Florida. Wind speeds reached 80 mph (130 kph); 14 people were killed, and around 1 million lost power to their homes.

PHOTOGRAPHER JIM REED CAUGHT IN THE STORM

AUG. 24
The tropical depression strengthened into a storm and was named Tropical Storm Katrina—the 11th named storm of 2005.

AUG. 26
The National Hurricane Center predicted that Katrina would head east toward the Gulf Coast. The governor of Louisiana declared a state of emergency.

AUG. 28 (7:00 AM)
Katrina strengthened into a Category 5 hurricane with wind speeds of up to 175 mph (280 kph).

8/23 8/24 8/25 8/26 8/27 8/28

AUG. 26
Hurricane Katrina weakened into a tropical storm, but started to grow again as it moved across the warm waters of the Gulf of Mexico.

AUG. 27
Katrina became a Category 3 hurricane. Authorities advised people to leave New Orleans. Roads were jammed as people fled the city.

AUG. 28 (7:00 AM)
The National Weather Service described Katrina as "potentially catastrophic."

AUG. 25 (5:00 PM)
Hurricane
Tropical Storm Katrina became a Category 1 hurricane, with wind speeds of 74–95 mph (119–153 kph).

SATELLITE IMAGE OF KATRINA

AUG. 28
Press conference
At a morning press conference, after Katrina was upgraded to a Category 5 hurricane, New Orleans mayor Ray Nagin ordered residents to evacuate the city.

EVACUATION ROUTE SIGN

> "WE ARE FACING A STORM THAT MOST OF US HAVE LONG FEARED."
> New Orleans mayor Ray Nagin

AUG. 28
Taking shelter
Those who had not been able to leave New Orleans took shelter in the Louisiana Superdome.
LINING UP OUTSIDE THE SUPERDOME

SEP. 1
Chaos in the city
New Orleans was in turmoil. Hundreds of people were trapped in their attics and on the rooftops of their homes—sometimes for several days. The US government sent in troops to provide relief.

FLOODED CITY STREETS

1.5 MILLION EVACUATED
from Louisiana

SEP. 4
Rescue
Thousands of troops and first responders poured into New Orleans to rescue survivors.
SAVING THE STRANDED

AUG. 30
Katrina weakened into a tropical storm and caused heavy rainfall in the state of Tennessee.

AUG. 31
Katrina became a tropical depression. Its remnants caused heavy rain in Canada.

| 8/29 | 8/30 | 8/31 | 9/1 | 9/2 | 9/4 | 2006 |

AUG. 31
In New Orleans, around 100,000 people were still stranded, and 25,000 were in the Superdome. Water levels stopped rising.

SEP. 2
Troops and supply trucks distributed food, clean drinking water, blankets, and first-aid kits.

SEP. 5
Floodwaters receded. However, most of New Orleans lay empty and in ruins.

AFTERMATH
The process of rebuilding the city of New Orleans began.

AUG. 29 (10:00 AM)
New Orleans
Winds up to 100 mph (160 kph) and heavy rain struck New Orleans. Levees (artificial banks that prevent flooding) failed. Water poured through the streets until 80 percent of the city was underwater. In some places it was 20 feet (6 m) deep.
SATELLITE VIEW OF FLOODING

2006 — **DRAWINGS BY DENISHA**
Survivor stories
Children who lived through Katrina related their experiences through stories and art. These pictures by Denisha show her house before and after the storm.

"BEFORE THE STORM, THERE WAS ALWAYS SOMETHING GOOD TO EAT ON OUR STOVE."
Denisha, Katrina's Kids Project

21

LIGHTNING STRIKES

Awesome and exciting, lightning is perhaps the most spectacular light show on Earth. Yet it can also be deadly. Every year, lightning injures about 240,000 people around the world and kills 24,000.

GLOBAL LIGHTNING

As you read this, there are about 1,800 thunderstorms taking place around the world. Warm regions get the most lightning—central Africa tops the list, followed by other places on or near the Equator.

LIGHTNING TYPES

There are different kinds of lightning. Some occur during the same storm. Heat from a lightning bolt sends shock waves through the air, making the crash of thunder.

Cloud to ground
This is the most common and deadly type of lightning. A bolt starts from a cloud, strikes the ground, then flashes back up the same path.

Cloud to cloud
In many thunderstorms, lightning flashes between clouds without touching the ground. If the bolts are obscured by the clouds, this type of lightning is known as sheet lightning.

Upper atmospheric
This type of lightning occurs far above thunderstorms. It includes red sprites, which flicker and dance in the air. It is usually faint and cannot be seen from the ground.

Hot spots
This image shows the concentration of lightning storms around the globe.

HOW IT WORKS

In a thunderstorm, water droplets in the clouds collide, giving them an electric charge. The charge builds up until there is a bolt of lightning, which connects the negative charge in the cloud to positive charges on the ground.

1

Charge builds up
Negative charges at the base of a thundercloud attract positive charges from the ground.

22 Disastrous Weather

Sparking a wildfire

Sparks from a bolt of lightning start a fire on the dry grasslands of South Africa. Minutes later, rain from the storm clouds extinguishes the fire before it can spread. Lightning is one of the main causes of wildfires.

270,000 mph (434,000 kph): the average speed of a LIGHTNING BOLT

EYEWITNESS

NAME: Steven Tufenk
DATE: June 29, 1991
LOCATION: St. Paul, MN
DETAILS: Steven Tufenk was struck by lightning while playing a round of golf.

"My friend putted and I putted and my ball went over next to his. . . . The next thing I knew my head hurt and I was hollerin' to my buddies that my head feels like it was going to explode. . . . 'I'm going down.' They said, 'Steve, relax, you're already on the ground, we were hit with lightning.' I didn't even know I was hit until my head felt like it was going to burst. I couldn't move. It threw me about 20 feet (6 m) through the air."

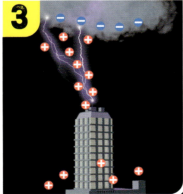

Leader stroke
...ing in short steps, a ...nel of negative charges, ...d a stepped leader stroke, ...ags its way to the ground.

Return stroke
When the negative and positive charges connect, lightning flashes back up to the cloud.

SURVIVORS' STORY

Nine out of every ten people struck by lightning in the US survive. However, many survivors often have problems afterward, such as stiff joints, blindness or sensitivity to light, hearing loss, memory loss, insomnia (inability to sleep), chronic pain, and difficulty sitting still for long periods at a time.

Struck seven times

US park ranger Roy Sullivan was struck by lightning a record-breaking seven times in 35 years—each time living to tell the tale.

23

BIG FREEZE

When the temperature drops, rain can be replaced by ice and snow. Snow looks beautiful, but the cold can kill. If the temperature falls below 5°F (–15°C), people caught outside risk frostbite or may even die of hypothermia.

SNOWSTORMS AND BLIZZARDS

Snowstorms form when freezing polar air meets warmer, more moist air. The heavier cold air forces the moist, warm air upward, where it deposits clouds of snowflakes, which then fall. A snowstorm becomes a blizzard when winds reach over 35 miles per hour (56 kph) and visibility is less than 1,300 feet (400 m).

Snow, sleet, or rain
Snow falls if the air is cold from the clouds to the ground. If cold and warm air meet, the result can be sleet or freezing rain.

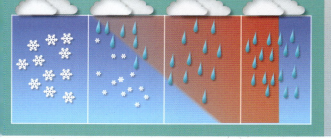

Dead end
Workers try to free a locomotive trapped between walls of snow in New York in 1888.

WORLD BLIZZARDS

In severe blizzards, icy winds whip snow along at speeds of over 45 miles per hour (72 kph), and visibility is reduced to zero. Blizzards are common in the United States and Canada, and they also occur in other mountainous countries, such as Iran and Afghanistan.

1888 — United States and Canada
In March 1888, the Great Blizzard dropped 4 feet (1.3 m) of snow over the eastern United States and Canada. Icy winds piled the snow into record-breaking drifts, some up to 50 feet (15 m) high. Over 400 people died.

1922 — United States
The Knickerbocker Storm hit the regions around Washington, DC, killing 98 people in the Knickerbocker Theatre, when the roof gave way under the snow.

Snowpocalypse

On January 23, 2016, New York City was buried in snow by the biggest blizzard since recordkeeping began there in 1869. Central Park disappeared under 27.5 inches (70 cm) of snow.

WHEN COLD KILLS

To work properly, your body temperature needs to stay at about 98.6°F (37°C). If it falls below this for too long, the result may be hypothermia.

98.6°F (37°C) Normal body temperature

96.8°F (36°C) Reduced body temperature: shivering

95.0°F (35°C) Mild hypothermia: numbness, drowsiness

89.6°F (32°C) Moderate hypothermia: difficulty moving

82.4°F (28°C) Severe hypothermia: loss of consciousness, possibly death

DANGER ABOVE

Icicles form when drops of water freeze, eventually creating long spikes of ice. These can be dangerous when they break off rooftops. In Russia, falling icicles killed five people in 2010.

Spears of ice

Icicles can be over 3 feet (1 m) long. They are more stable in freezing weather but may fall when the air warms up.

1972

Iran
Around 4,000 people died during the deadliest blizzard on record. Winds dumped as much as 26 feet (8 m) of snow on some villages, burying all of the inhabitants.

1993

United States and Canada
This blizzard was nicknamed the "Storm of the Century" because of its huge snowfall and hurricane-force winds. It killed over 300 people, mainly due to hypothermia.

2008

Afghanistan
During this blizzard, the third deadliest on record, 926 people died in mountainous parts of the country. Up to 6.5 feet (2 m) of snow fell and temperatures dropped as low as −13°F (−25°C).

2022

United States
In December 2022, a 2,000-mile- (3220-km-) wide storm reaching from Texas to Maine knocked out power to more than 1.4 million homes. The storm killed at least 100 people.

25

AVALANCHE!

Snow may look harmless, but it can kill if it suddenly starts to slide downhill. Within seconds, it can move at up to 80 miles per hour (130 kph), burying anything in its path.

TYPES OF AVALANCHE

No two avalanches are the same, but three common types are loose snow, slab, and cornice avalanches. All types of avalanches are most common in the early spring, when warm air melts and loosens packed snow.

MOUNTAIN DANGER

In February 2015, unprecedented avalanches caused by heavy winter snow engulfed northeastern provinces of Afghanistan. They killed at least 286 people, most in the province of Panjshir. After the avalanche, people stood on rooftops waiting to be rescued.

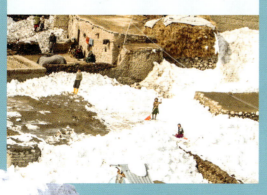

Loose snow
Loose, powdery snow starts to roll down a slope in a widening fan shape.

Release point
These avalanches often start from a point like a tree.

Slab
An entire layer of snow begins to move, breaking up into pieces as it heads downhill.

Giant slabs
Chunks can be the size of cars.

Wind direction

Cornice
Snow blown by the wind builds up on a ridge. The overhanging snow then breaks at the fracture zone, tumbling down the slope below.

Fracture zone

Overhanging snow

26 Disastrous Weather

SURVIVAL

Carrying a survival pack can save your life or help you rescue another person. It contains an inflatable air bag and a shovel to use if you are trapped in snow. A probe locates victims so that rescuers know where to dig. The transceiver broadcasts a radio signal. When set to receive mode, it can pinpoint the signal of someone who is buried in snow.

PROTECTION

Skiers and snowboarders are warned if there is a risk of an avalanche. Villages are protected through blasting and by erecting barriers.

Blasting
Explosives dislodge snow in a controlled way.

Barriers
Netting and wooden barriers can stop small snowslides.

EYEWITNESS

NAME: Ian Measeck
DATE: February 27, 2010
LOCATION: New York
DETAILS: Ian Measeck of Glens Falls, NY, was caught in an avalanche while skiing down Wright Peak.

" The sensation is best described as almost instant acceleration in a river of wet cement. I was suddenly surrounded by this flowing snowbank. . . . I don't remember much aside from the dark, the fear, and the thought that I had to try to stay on top of it somehow. "

Tumbling snow
Visitors at the Mount Foraker base camp in Denali National Park, in Alaska, watch snow tumble down the mountainside.

90% of **AVALANCHES** that involve people are **TRIGGERED** by the victim or someone nearby.

WILDFIRES

Raging across grasslands or through forests, wildfires can spread quickly across the countryside, bringing disaster to anyone caught in their paths. They spread fastest in hot weather, when vegetation is dry.

SPARKING A WILDFIRE

Some wildfires spark naturally from a bolt of lightning. Others are caused when fires lit to clear land for farming get out of control. Most start through human carelessness—such as a discarded cigarette butt.

The fire triangle

A wildfire needs oxygen and fuel to make it burn, as well as a source of ignition.

Ignition — This provides the initial source of heat, which lights the fuel.

Fuel — Fuels include wood, grass, brush, and peat (soil made of rotted vegetation).

Oxygen — Oxygen reacts with the fuel, releasing large amounts of heat.

HOW FIRE SPREADS

Wildfires spread rapidly if there is a large fuel supply and hot, windy weather to fan the flames. Winds usually blow up hills since warm air rises. So fires rage upward on sloping ground.

Fuel supply

Weather

Type of land

FANNING THE FLAMES

Fires are a natural feature of dry forests and scrubland—some plants even depend on the heat to release their seeds. However, the number of fires is steadily on the rise. Over three-quarters of all wildfires are started by humans. Each year, there are more than 70,000 wildfires in the United States alone.

Surviving the flames

This Australian banksia has adapted to withstand periodic, naturally occurring wildfires, only releasing its seeds when scorched.

CHARRED SEED CONE

DEADLY WILDFIRES

Wildfires have caused a number of major disasters over the last 150 years. Most have struck forests, but some have destroyed cities and towns. In the past, when buildings were often made of wood and fire services were limited, hundreds of people sometimes perished in the flames.

1871

United States

On October 8, fire broke out in Chicago, Illinois. During the blaze, 90,000 people lost their homes. Strong winds blew burning embers into the center of the city, helping the fire spread.

Disastrous Weather

PUTTING OUT FIRES

Firefighters use different techniques to control a blaze. Special planes drop water and fire-retardant chemicals. Smoke jumpers parachute into remote areas near the advancing flames to clear brush, cutting off a fire's fuel supply.

Superscooper
The Canadair CL-215 scoops water from lakes and reservoirs, then drops it on wildfires. It can carry 1,320 gallons (5,000 L) at a time.

Smoke jumper
One of the very first smoke jumpers prepares to leap from a plane during a blaze in Oregon in 1945.

EYEWITNESS

NAME: Unknown
DATE: February 7, 2009
LOCATION: Warrandyte, Victoria, Australia
DETAILS: This eyewitness was one of the crew on a North Warrandyte fire truck (Strike Team 1364) battling to put out the Black Saturday wildfires.

" We tried to stop the fire [from] jumping a road, but it was impossible. The fire. . . . raced through the forest, destroying houses and killing people inside. "

Emergency escape
Threatened by the flames, a fire truck rushes for safety during Australia's Black Saturday, in February 2009. These bushfires killed 173 people and injured more than 400.

1936 — **1987** — **2009** — **2018** — **2023**

Soviet Union
The Kursha-2 settlement, built to house workers who were chopping down local forests, was destroyed in a wildfire. Around 1,200 people died.

China and the Soviet Union
The Black Dragon Fire, one of the biggest wildfires of recent times, burned 18 million acres (7 million ha) of forest around the Amur River.

Australia
In Victoria, the Black Saturday bushfires killed 173 people and injured over 400. It was the worst recorded wildfire disaster in the state's history.

Greece
Fanned by hot winds and encouraged by drought, forest fires blazed in several areas of Greece. The fires killed at least 104 people.

United States
Very dry and windy conditions resulted in wildfires that spread through Lahaina, Maui, killing at least 97. More than 2,200 buildings were damaged or destroyed.

UNSTABLE EARTH

FIND OUT

?

WHAT is pahoehoe lava?
WHERE did deadly earthquakes strike in 2023?
HOW can we predict an earthquake?

LANDSLIDES

We take solid ground for granted, but disaster can strike if it starts to slip and slide. Some landslides are slow and gradual. The most dangerous ones happen quickly, without warning, making it difficult to escape.

MUDSLIDE DISASTERS
Steep slopes and crowded housing can be a dangerous mix. During storms, heavy rain can start to move the soil in a muddy mass that overwhelms anything (or anybody) in its path as it sweeps downhill.

Giant rockfall
Watched by a solitary figure, a giant rockfall crashes into a valley in northeast Pakistan in January 2010. A few weeks earlier, an even larger landslide in the same area blocked the Hunza River. It formed a new lake that flooded farmland and submerged villages, forcing 30,000 people to move.

CAUSE AND EFFECT
Frost and rain often loosen slopes, making soil unstable. People also cause landslides by cutting down trees, which have roots holding the earth in place. Some landslides are caused by earthquakes or volcanic activity.

Types of movement
Landslides range from slow soil creep to rockfalls in which the forces holding a slope together suddenly give way.

1

Soil creep
Soil slowly edges downhill as it freezes and thaws.

2

Slumping
The ground slides in curved slabs, forming giant terraces, or steps.

32 Unstable Earth

WASHINGTON, US, 2014, 43 KILLED

SIERRA LEONE, AUGUST 2017, 1,100+ KILLED

BRAZIL, FEBRUARY 2022, 231 KILLED

The fastest landslides move at **100 feet (30 m)** **A SECOND!**

3

4

5

Debris slide
Rocks shattered by frost race down the side of a mountain.

Mudflow
Mud pours downhill after a heavy rain.

Rockfall
Rocks plummet to the ground as a slope collapses.

33

RESTLESS EARTH

Many natural disasters happen because Earth's outer layer, or crust, is moving. Huge blocks of crust called plates collide or separate, causing earthquakes and volcanic eruptions where they meet or pull apart.

MOBILE CRUST

Earth's plates "float" on the magma, or molten rock, below the crust. Magma flows like thick tar, moving the plates about 0.5 inches (1.3 cm) a year.

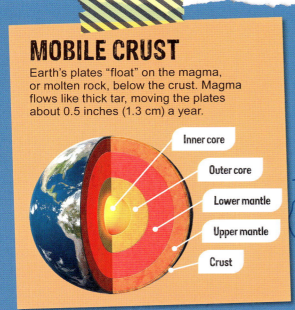

1 SUNDHNÚKSGÍGAR ERUPTION
Iceland

The country of Iceland lies on the Mid-Atlantic Ridge, where two plates are diverging, or pulling apart. Volcanic activity, such as the eruption at Sundhnúksgígar in 2024, is common at divergent boundaries.

2 KAIKOURA EARTHQUAKE
New Zealand

Parts of New Zealand lie over transform boundaries, where two plates may suddenly slip or slide past each other. The 2016 earthquake in Kaikoura triggered landslides that cut the town off from the rest of the South Island.

Plates, boundaries, and faults

Earth has 7 large plates and about 40 smaller ones that meet at boundaries. Fault lines mark the giant cracks in Earth's crust at these boundaries. The world's most active fault surrounds the Pacific plate. It is a "ring of fire" because of the volcanoes all along its edge. The San Andreas Fault, which lies between the Pacific and North American plates, is also highly active.

TYPES OF BOUNDARIES

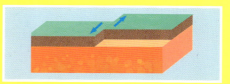

Transform boundaries
At transform boundaries, Earth's plates grind past one another, causing earthquakes.

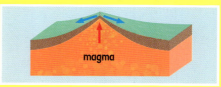

Divergent boundaries
At divergent boundaries, magma pushed up from the mantle creates new crust that moves two plates apart, forming ridges.

Convergent boundaries
At convergent boundaries, plates collide. Heavier crust buckles as it is forced below a lighter plate. This collision causes powerful earthquakes. Magma may also be forced upward at the edges of the plates and form volcanoes.

3 CALBUCO ERUPTION
Chile
In 2015, Mount Calbuco, in Chile, erupted and shot lava 9 miles (15 km) above its crater. Like many volcanoes, it lies close to a convergent boundary, where two plates collide.

4 YELLOWSTONE GEYSER
United States
Despite being far from a boundary or a fault line, Yellowstone's springs and geysers are heated by "hot spots." Magma rises to just below the surface, making a bulge and causing volcanic activity.

EARTH SCIENTISTS

Geologists, or earth scientists, are on the front line of research about natural disasters. Some risk their lives to study active volcanoes. Others investigate earthquakes to learn how and when they may next strike.

PARKFIELD CASE STUDY

The town of Parkfield, California, sits on the San Andreas Fault. It bristles with seismological instruments—it is the best-studied earthquake zone in the world. At Parkfield, scientists measure the way that the ground creeps along the fault, where two neighboring plates meet.

Laser monitoring
At Parkfield, instruments called Geodimeters aim laser beams across the fault. The beams bounce back from reflectors, and computers measure how long they take to return. Any change in time taken is caused by movement in the rocks along the fault.

Creep meter
A creep meter calculates fault slip (how the rocks move in relation to one another). The meter measures the distance between two piers placed in the ground. The piers are connected by a wire. Any movements in the wire are measured by electronic gauges.

Strainmeter
Strainmeters monitor tiny deformations in Earth's crust due to fault slips, earthquakes, and volcanic activity. Powered by solar panels, strainmeters can be completely automatic. They send data to satellites, and the data is then transmitted to computers on Earth for analysis.

San Andreas Fault
Seen from the air, the San Andreas Fault looks like a gigantic scar slicing across the land. In this view, near Parkfield, the edge of the Pacific plate is on the left, and the edge of the North American plate is on the right.

Seismologists
Seismologists study all kinds of earthquakes, from tiny ground tremors to huge jolts. One of their jobs is to examine the way that forces build up below the ground before quakes occur. This may help them warn people that a quake is going to hit. This trace from a seismograph shows ground movement during a quake.

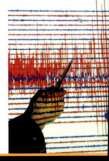

Dancing with death
A volcanologist records lava flowing from Mount Etna, on the Italian island of Sicily. When it solidifies, the lava will form the black rock that surrounds the flow. Etna is the largest active volcano in Europe, and one of the world's most studied volcanoes.

Volcanologists at work
Volcanologists are like detectives. They track down clues from volcanic rocks or gases to predict future eruptions and perhaps save lives. Their work sometimes takes them right to the edge of an exploding volcano, where dangers may include inhaling poisonous gas or being injured by red-hot lava.

In the field
In a protective suit that reflects heat, a scientist uses a pickax to take a sample of lava back to the laboratory for analysis.

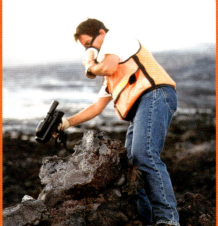

Radar gun
A volcanologist uses a radar gun to measure the speed of lava flow beneath surface rocks. The gun is similar to those used to measure the speed of a baseball as it is pitched.

EARTHQUAKES

Earthquakes happen with little warning, so there is almost no time for people to react. For a few terrifying minutes, the ground shakes violently, sometimes bringing buildings crashing down.

TYPES OF EARTHQUAKES

Earthquakes occur along faults in Earth's crust, at plate margins. They happen when neighboring plates move. Sometimes, moving plates get stuck, causing energy to build up until it is suddenly released in an earthquake.

Normal faults
These are found at divergent boundaries, where one plate drops relative to the other. Resulting earthquakes vary in strength. The Papua New Guinea quake in 2022 was magnitude 7.6.

Thrust faults
These are found at convergent boundaries, where one plate is pushed below the other. The result is an earthquake and sometimes a tsunami. An example is the 1960 Chilean earthquake.

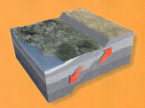

Strike-slip faults
These are found at transform boundaries, where one plate slides past another. The result can range from minor tremors to a huge earthquake, such as the quakes that shook Turkey and Syria in 2023.

Seismic waves
These waves of energy spread out from the hypocenter.

Epicenter
Most damage occurs at the epicenter—the point on Earth's surface directly above the hypocenter.

Hypocenter
The hypocenter, or focus, is where the rock fractures.

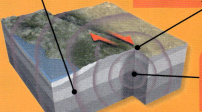

Twisted tracks
Workers assess damage to a railroad track after a huge earthquake hit Christchurch, New Zealand, in 2010.

38 Unstable Earth

MOMENT MAGNITUDE SCALE

The Moment Magnitude Scale measures an earthquake's magnitude, or size and strength. Each step up represents a tenfold increase, so a quake that measures 8 shakes the ground 1,000 times more than a quake that measures 5.

8 or more — Serious damage over extensive area

7 Major — Serious damage over large area

6 Strong — Great damage near epicenter

5.5 Moderate — Some damage near epicenter

2.5 Light — Usually felt, damage rare

1 Minor — Often not felt, but can be detected by a seismograph

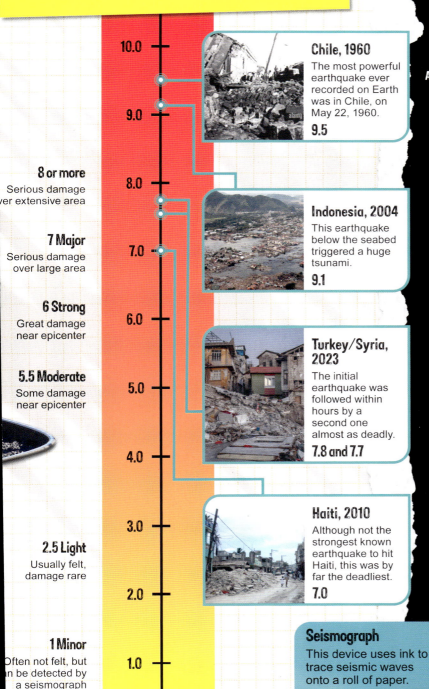

Chile, 1960
The most powerful earthquake ever recorded on Earth was in Chile, on May 22, 1960.
9.5

Indonesia, 2004
This earthquake below the seabed triggered a huge tsunami.
9.1

Turkey/Syria, 2023
The initial earthquake was followed within hours by a second one almost as deadly.
7.8 and 7.7

Haiti, 2010
Although not the strongest known earthquake to hit Haiti, this was by far the deadliest.
7.0

Seismograph
This device uses ink to trace seismic waves onto a roll of paper.

DEADLY EARTHQUAKES

Throughout history, earthquakes striking populated regions have killed millions of people. On the other hand, the most powerful earthquake ever recorded, in Chile in 1960, caused fewer deaths (around 5,000) because it struck an area with a low population.

AD 526	**Antakya, Turkey**	250,000 killed; magnitude unknown
865	**Damghan, Iran**	200,000 killed; magnitude unknown
1138	**Aleppo, Syria**	230,000 killed; magnitude unknown
1556	**China**	830,000 killed; magnitude 8.0
1727	**Tabriz, Iran**	77,000 killed; magnitude 7.7
1908	**Messina, Italy**	72,000 killed; magnitude 7.5
1923	**Kanto, Japan**	142,800 killed; magnitude 7.9
1948	**Ashgabat, Turkmenistan**	110,000 killed; magnitude 7.3
1976	**Tangshan, China**	242,769 killed; magnitude 7.5
2004	**Sumatra, Indonesia**	227,898 killed; magnitude 9.1
2010	**Port-au-Prince, Haiti**	316,000 killed; magnitude 7.0
2015	**Nepal**	9,000 killed; magnitude 7.8
2018	**Palu, Indonesia**	4,340 killed; magnitude 7.4
2023	**Turkey/Syria**	55,000+ killed; magnitudes 7.8 and 7.7

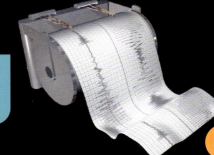

39

ALL IN RUINS

On Monday, February 6, 2023, a deadly magnitude 7.8 earthquake struck south central Turkey and northern Syria. Just nine hours later, another earthquake struck that was magnitude 7.7. By March 1, there had been more than 11,000 aftershocks. An area the size of Germany was devastated, almost 60,000 people died, and millions were displaced.

AFTERMATH OF AN EARTHQUAKE

On February 6, 2023, a series of powerful earthquakes shook southern Turkey near the border with Syria. They were the most damaging quakes to hit the region in 20 years, killing almost 60,000 people and leaving many more homeless.

FEB 6 (4:17 AM LOCAL TIME)
Deadly earthquake
A magnitude 7.8 earthquake struck near Gaziantep in south-central Turkey. It occurred along the East Anatolian Fault, a strike-slip fault where the Anatolian and Arabian tectonic plates slide past each other.

FEB 6 (1:24 PM LOCAL TIME)
A magnitude 7.7 aftershock shook the same region.

FEB 6
Rescuers began to dig survivors out of the rubble and help people shelter from the freezing winter conditions.

FEB 6
Nearby countries such as Lebanon and Azerbaijan sent emergency services to help with the rescue effort. People in Turkey also called for aid on social media.

FEB 6 (8:00 PM)
Huge casualties
The casualties in Turkey and Syria had already reached over 4,000 people. Many more people were injured.

FEB 7 (12:00 AM)
The Turkish and Syrian Red Crescent organizations distributed blankets, mattresses, and hot meals as temperatures dropped overnight. They also transported people to hospitals.

FEB 7 (4:00 PM)
The president of Turkey declared a state of emergency in 10 provinces.

FEB 6
Historic sites
Many ancient buildings were badly damaged, including the 2,000-year-old Gaziantep Castle. Its walls collapsed during the first quake.

GAZIANTEP CASTLE RUINS

FEB 7 (10:00 PM)
Search and rescue
Search-and-rescue teams, sniffer dogs, and equipment arrived from 19 countries in the European Union, as well as the UK, Albania, and Montenegro.

SNIFFER DOG SEARCHES FOR TRAPPED VICTIMS

42 Unstable Earth

FEB 7 (10:00 PM)
Buildings destroyed
The United Nations announced that about 6,000 buildings in Turkey were damaged or destroyed and at least 250,000 people were homeless.

COLLAPSED BUILDINGS IN KAHRAMANMARAŞ PROVINCE

FEB 18
Survivor story
Hakan Yasinoglu had been trapped under a flattened building for 11 days. Rescue workers pulled him from the rubble, and he was reunited via video call with his baby daughter, who was born just hours before the first earthquake hit.

FEB 8
About 8,000 people had been rescued from collapsed buildings in Turkey.

FEB 19
Turkey announced the end of search-and-rescue efforts in most of the hardest-hit provinces.

2/8 — 2/9 — 2/14 — 2/18 — 2/19 — 2024

FEB 8 (12:00 PM)
The total number of aftershocks reached almost 650.

FEB 9
The first international aid organizations entered Syria. Rescue efforts were delayed by the ongoing civil war in the country.

FEB 14
A dam collapsed in northwestern Syria and caused the Orontes River to flood. Thousands of people were forced to evacuate their homes.

MARCH
Pledges of foreign financial aid reached more than $7.5 billion.

FEB 8 (1:00 PM)
International support
The United States increased its support, sending 100 Californian firefighters to join search-and-rescue teams from China, India, Mexico, Russia, and the Middle East.

2024
One year later
Turkey and Syria still faced a long road to recovery. Much of the region was still in ruins and thousands of people were living in tent cities. Many of them were Syrian refugees, who fled to Turkey to escape the civil war before the earthquakes hit.

TENT CITY HOUSES EARTHQUAKE VICTIMS

43

LIVING WITH EARTHQUAKES

Scientists can detect earthquakes, but they still cannot predict when or where the next big one will strike. That is why it is important to be prepared when you live in, or are visiting, an earthquake zone.

Taipei 101 tower

EARTHQUAKE PREDICTION

The first known earthquake detector was made in China, in AD 132. It showed that a quake had occurred, and from which direction. Modern seismometers are more precise. Working in groups, they pinpoint earthquakes thousands of miles away.

Ancient detector

The old Chinese detector held eight bronze balls. When it shook, one of the dragons dropped a ball into the frog's open mouth below.

Dragon releases ball in quake

Modern seismometer

Some digital seismometers are designed specifically for use on the seabed, where an earthquake may cause a tsunami.

EARTHQUAKE PROTECTION

Some of the world's tallest buildings stand in earthquake zones. They are protected from damage during an earthquake by shock-absorbing foundations and tuned mass dampers, which work like giant pendulums.

Taipei 101

This record-breaking building is over 1,640 feet (500 m) tall. Its main pendulum, suspended between the 87th and 92nd floors, weighs as much as two fully loaded jumbo jets.

101 pendulum

The pendulum at the top of the tower swings during tremors or strong winds, absorbing energy that could otherwise make the building collapse.

Unstable Earth

10,000: the average number of people who die in EARTHQUAKES each year

EYEWITNESS

NAME: Yukiko
DATE: March 11, 2011
LOCATION: Tokyo, Japan
DETAILS: Office worker Yukiko posted this message online shortly after the Tohoku earthquake struck off the Japanese coast.

> Although we're far from northern Japan, the quake here was very big. The first quake was very long—everyone in the office was screaming. Then we had another long one about 30 minutes after that. Paper and items were falling off the desks. . . . We can hear the walls going back and forth.

EARTHQUAKE DRILL

In the Philippine capital of Manila, children cover their heads with padded hoods as part of a regular earthquake drill. The children need to be prepared because the islands that make up the Philippines lie on the Pacific Ring of Fire—the world's most earthquake-prone region.

STRATOVOLCANOES

While you are reading this, about 20 volcanoes are erupting in different places around the world. The most dangerous kinds are giant stratovolcanoes, which can blast ash and gas high into Earth's atmosphere.

LIFE CYCLE OF A VOLCANO

Most active stratovolcanoes are less than 100,000 years old. A stratovolcano is particularly dangerous during the first part of its life cycle, when it can reach a gigantic size. Eventually, its eruptions become less frequent. Finally, they stop altogether, and the volcano becomes extinct.

Ash and gas cloud
Winds carry volcanic ash far away. Volcanoes also give off poisonous gases that mix in the atmosphere.

Lava flow
Lava streams from the vents down the volcano's sides, turning solid when it cools.

Lava field

Cone
Stratovolcanoes usually have tall, symmetrical cones.

Strata

Main vent
Magma wells up through this vent and pours out of the opening at the top of the cone.

Secondary vent
Large volcanoes often have smaller secondary vents.

Conduit
This passageway connects the magma chamber to the volcano's vents.

Magma

1 Birth
A stratovolcano starts life when magma, or molten rock, forces its way upward from a chamber deep underground. The volcano erupts each time magma wells up to the surface. Magma that has erupted from a volcano is called lava.

2 Active period
Layers of ash and lava, called strata, form with each eruption, building up into a tall, steep-sided cone. The volcano grows rapidly, until it may be over 16,400 feet (5,000 m) high. A field of lava spreads out from its base, creating a desolate landscape with few signs of life.

Unstable Earth

VESUVIUS ERUPTION

In AD 79, Mount Vesuvius in Italy erupted, covering nearby Herculaneum and Pompeii in a 13-foot (4-m) layer of burning pumice and ash. Following the rediscovery of the buried cities in 1748, people made plaster casts of the victims' bodies using the hollows left in the hardened ash after the bodies decomposed.

EYEWITNESS

NAME: Pliny the Younger
DATE: After AD 79
LOCATION: Misenum, Italy
DETAILS: Pliny, who was staying with his uncle near Vesuvius, later wrote letters describing what happened during the eruption.

" Ashes were already falling. . . . I looked round: a dense black cloud was coming up behind us, spreading over the earth like a flood. . . . Ashes began to fall again, this time in heavy showers. We rose from time to time and shook them off, otherwise we should have been buried and crushed beneath their weight. "

VOLCANIC FALLOUT

When a volcano erupts, billions of rocky particles are blasted into the air. The heaviest fragments soon drop to the ground, but specks of ash can be blown great distances by strong winds.

Ash
Particles of ash are less than 0.08 inches (2 mm) across. A dense ash cloud can blot out the Sun.

Ash particle
Sharp edges are dangerous if ash gets into eyes or airplane engines.

Lapilli
Measuring 0.08–2.5 inches (2–64 mm) across, lapilli look like tiny stones. They turn from molten to solid rock as they fall.

Bombs
Fragments over 2.5 inches (64 mm) drop near the vent.

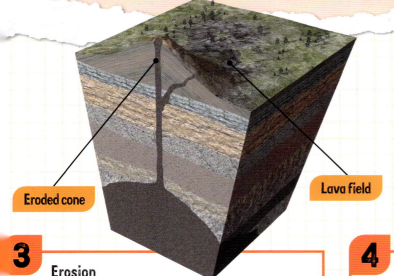

Eroded cone

Lava field

3 Erosion
When the volcano is no longer active, erosion takes over. Wind and rain eat away at the hardened ash, and the cone and the lava field shrink in size. Plants grow in cracks in the lava, nourished by the fertile volcanic soil.

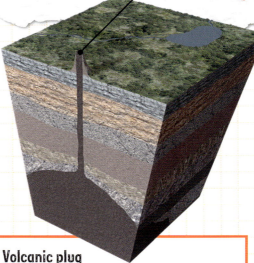

Plug of solid magma

4 Volcanic plug
After many thousands of years, the lava field is still visible, but most of the cone has eroded away. The only part left is a tall "plug"—the core of hardened magma from the volcano's main conduit.

47

LAVA AND LAHARS

When a volcano erupts, lava flows down its slopes, destroying everything in its path. Just as dangerous are lahars—mudflows of melting snow and ice, volcanic ash, and debris that pour down in a gray torrent at high speeds.

TYPES OF LAVA

PAHOEHOE LAVA

Pahoehoe lava is thin and runny, with a glassy skin. It forms a smooth surface when it cools and becomes solid.

AA LAVA

Aa lava is stickier than pahoehoe lava and has a rough surface when it solidifies.

PILLOW LAVA

Pillow lava forms on the seabed like toothpaste being squeezed out of a tube.

LAVA BOMB

Lava bombs are lumps of molten rock thrown up into the air during an eruption on land.

LAVA ON THE MOVE

In May 2018, an eruption of the Kilauea volcano changed the island of Hawaii forever. Huge, fluid lava flows moved very quickly downhill, covered the land, and swallowed everything in their paths until they reached the ocean. The lava flows eventually stopped in early August. Kilauea remains highly active. It has erupted every year since 2020 and more volcanic activity is expected in the future.

RELENTLESS FLOW

On the Big Island of Hawaii, 716 homes were completely destroyed by lava flows from Kilauea. Some 3,000 people were displaced, roads became impassable, and the damage to forests and farms was devastating.

49

VOLCANO FACTS

There are around 1,300–1,500 active volcanoes on Earth, and many more are either dormant (inactive) or extinct. But appearances can be deceiving. After thousands of years in a deep "sleep," dormant volcanoes can suddenly erupt, bringing disaster to those living nearby.

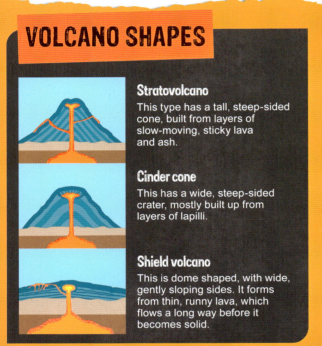

VOLCANO SHAPES

Stratovolcano
This type has a tall, steep-sided cone, built from layers of slow-moving, sticky lava and ash.

Cinder cone
This has a wide, steep-sided crater, mostly built up from layers of lapilli.

Shield volcano
This is dome shaped, with wide, gently sloping sides. It forms from thin, runny lava, which flows a long way before it becomes solid.

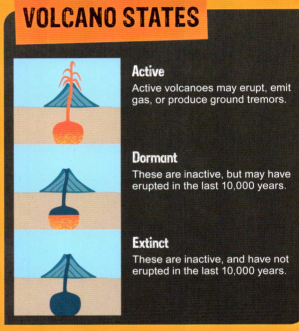

VOLCANO STATES

Active
Active volcanoes may erupt, emit gas, or produce ground tremors.

Dormant
These are inactive, but may have erupted in the last 10,000 years.

Extinct
These are inactive, and have not erupted in the last 10,000 years.

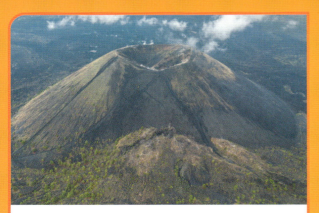

Fast-growing volcano
In February 1943, Parícutin volcano burst to life in a cornfield in Mexico. It grew to 1,391 feet (424 m) tall in just 9 years.

Loudest noise
In 1883, the volcanic island of Krakatau, Indonesia, exploded, producing the loudest sound ever recorded on Earth. Just 4.5 hours after the initial explosion, the sound was herd in Perth, Australia, 2,200 miles (3,540 km) away.

DEADLY VOLCANOES

Here are 10 of the highest known death tolls from volcanoes in history. Five followed eruptions in Indonesia.

- **10** — 3,500 Vesuvius (Italy) 1631
- **9** — 4,000 Galunggung (Indonesia) 1882
- **8** — 5,000 Kelud (Indonesia) 1919
- **7** — 9,000 Laki (Iceland) 1783
- **6** — 10,000 Kelud (Indonesia) 1586
- **5** — 15,000 Unzen (Japan) 1792
- **4** — 25,000 Nevado Del Ruiz (Colombia) 1985
- **3** — 29,000 Mont Pelée (Martinique) 1902
- **2** — 36,000 Krakatau (Indonesia) 1883
- **1** — 92,000 Tambora (Indonesia) 1815

Death toll
The highest number of known deaths from an eruption occurred in 1815, when Mount Tambora exploded in Indonesia. People died in the eruption itself and from famine after ash smothered farm animals and crops.

BIGGEST VOLCANOES
The biggest volcano in our solar system is Olympus Mons, on Mars. On land, Earth's tallest volcano is Ojos del Salado. However, if measured from their bases on the seafloor, the tallest volcanoes are Mauna Kea and neighboring Mauna Loa on the island of Hawaii.

THE TALLEST VOLCANOES

Olympus Mons
82,000 ft (25,000 m)
Olympus Mons is an enormous shield volcano that could easily swallow up Earth's 10 biggest volcanoes with room to spare.

Highest from sea level
22,615 ft (6,893 m)
Ojos del Salado is a stratovolcano located at the border between Argentina and Chile.

Highest from seafloor
13,796 ft (4,205 m)
Mauna Kea is a huge shield volcano on the island of Hawaii.

Runner-up
13,678 ft (4,169 m)
Mauna Loa is the second highest volcano on Earth if measured from the seafloor.

AFTERMATH OF THE MAGNITUDE 9.0 EARTHQUAKE AND TSUNAMI, SENDAI, JAPAN, 2011

TROUBLED WATER

FIND OUT

WHERE was the worst flood in history?
WHICH country suffers from the most extreme monsoons?
WHICH disaster struck on December 26, 2004?

53

FLOODING

Floods can kill tens of thousands of people every year. Most floods occur after prolonged, heavy rain when waterlogged ground can no longer absorb water and gives way, often causing landslides or mudslides. In 2022, flooding brought disaster around the world. The worst floods occurred in Pakistan, affecting one-third of the country.

United States

In a period of 11 days during the summer of 2022, the US had four major flooding events. Death Valley in California, known for searing heat, had almost a year's worth of rain—1.7 inches (4.4 cm)—in just three hours.

Nigeria

In September 2022, unusually heavy rains engulfed the country in floodwaters that affected 34 of its 36 states. More than 1 million people were left homeless, and farms and harvests across the country were destroyed.

Brazil

In 2022, in some regions, 70 percent of the rain expected for the whole month of December fell in less than 24 hours. This caused catastrophic flash floods and landslides that led to 25,000 people losing their homes.

United States

Flash floods hit the Southwest, closing highways in Colorado, submerging cars in Texas, and trapping tourists in a cave in New Mexico.

NORTH AMERICA

California

Portugal
In December, flash floods swept through the streets of Lisbon, Portugal's capital city.

NIGERIA

BRAZIL

SOUTH AMERICA

RIVER FLOODING

For thousands of years, people have lived close to rivers or on low-lying land near coasts. This land is often rich and fertile, but there is a price to pay. Days or weeks of rain can cause rivers and lakes to overflow, and the strength of a raging torrent of water can easily wash away roads, bridges, and homes.

How rivers flood

If the ground is saturated, rainwater runs across its surface, flooding flat land or filling rivers and lakes until they overflow.

Troubled Water

Flood protection

Floods cause so much damage that governments spend time and money on flood protection. Emergency warnings give people time to prepare or evacuate homes. Dams such as the Three Gorges Dam on the Yangtze River, in China, hold back floodwater, releasing it in a controlled way to prevent flooding.

Pakistan

The 2022 summer monsoon season brought months of rainfall, floods, and landslides. More than one-third of the country was inundated, with 1,739 people killed and 33 million people (1 in 7 of the population) displaced.

South Africa

A national state of disaster was declared in April 2022 after intense rain caused landslides and flooding that destroyed homes and roads. About 540 people lost their lives and 142,000 people were displaced from their communities.

Australia

A series of floods in eastern Australia from February to April 2022 was followed by an extremely wet October. The saturated soil and full dams led to even more flooding across New South Wales and Victoria when new storms came.

Southern Europe
Torrential rain caused severe flooding across southern Europe in September.

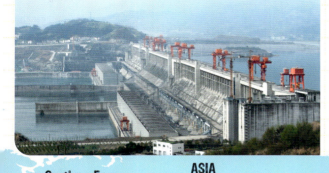

1. Heavy rain falls on waterlogged ground.
2. Runoff pours downhill.
3. River rises rapidly, flooding the valley floor.

The deadliest flood EVER recorded on Earth:

150,000 KILLED

Huang He River, China, 1931

MONSOON FLOODS

In regions with a monsoon climate, such as southern Asia and western Africa, the long dry season is followed by months of torrential rain. The rain is vital for growing crops, but it can spell disaster if rivers overflow their banks, flooding villages and towns.

HOW MONSOONS WORK

During the summer monsoon, or wet season, the wind blows inland, picking up moisture as it crosses the warm waters of the ocean. The moisture falls as rain over the land. The wind changes direction six months later during the dry winter monsoon.

Winter monsoon
In the dry season, the Sun is lower in the sky. The land cools down, and dry winds blow out to sea.

- Cool air from mountain regions
- Cool, dry winds

Rain from humid wind condensed over land

Warm air, moist from evaporated seawater

Warm land, drawing in air from the sea

Summer monsoon
In the wet season, the Sun is high in the sky, heating up the land. The moisture-filled monsoon wind blows inland from the sea, bringing heavy rain.

56 Troubled Water

Flooded streets
A woman and child make their way through the flooded streets of Kolkata, India, during the 2018 monsoon.

MONSOONS IN ASIA
During the wet summer months, rivers burst their banks and drainage systems often overflow, flooding streets and homes. South and Southeast Asia experience the world's most extreme monsoons.

China, 2020
During China's most severe monsoon season for 60 years, the Yangtze River Basin flooded five times, affecting millions of people across the country.

Pakistan, 2022
Monsoon rainfall in Pakistan in 2022 was three times higher than usual. Flooding and landslides displaced more than 30 million people.

Nepal, 2024
Flooding blocked major roads and bridges in Kathmandu during the summer monsoon season.

EYEWITNESS
NAME: Alamzeb
DATE: August 2010
LOCATION: Pakistan
DETAILS: Alamzeb and his relatives were trapped by monsoon flooding in Nowshera, Pakistan.

"We never thought the waters would rise so high. I was away at my aunt's house in the Nowshera Cantonment area. When the waters overflowed the river, I got worried. My relatives said to wait until the tide ebbs, but it kept rising, and soon it was clear that my part of the city had drowned.

My mother died. She was old and diabetic and couldn't climb to the third floor of the house to avoid drowning. My younger brother, who is only 12, tried to drag her up. She was washed away. We haven't found her body. My brother is traumatized."

366 inches: (930 cm)
July rainfall in Cherrapunji, India, the wettest place on Earth

TSUNAMIS

Most waves are caused when the wind blows across the surface of the sea. Tsunamis are bigger and much more dangerous. These immense waves are set in motion by earthquakes under the seafloor.

HOW A TSUNAMI FORMS

An earthquake below the seabed causes seafloor rocks to shift. This movement pushes up an immense ridge of water. The water spreads out in all directions as waves, which can travel across the open ocean as fast as a passenger plane.

1 Seabed shifts
Two neighboring plates shift during an earthquake. One plate pushes upward, creating a short-lived ridge of water at the surface.

0 sec.

2 Tsunami begins
Pulled down by gravity, the ridge collapses, triggering a series of waves. The waves race outward, like ripples from a pebble thrown into a pond.

20 sec.

3 Crossing the ocean
The deeper the water, the faster the tsunami travels. In the deep open ocean, the waves can reach speeds of up to 500 mph (800 kph).

30 min.

Ridge of water
Although not tall, the ridge can be more than 620 miles (1,000 km) long.

DART warning buoy

Ocean waves
In open water, the waves are short in height and spread far apart.

Earthquake hypocenter, or focus

Earthquake epicenter

Seabed earthquake detector

58 Troubled Water

1,720 (524 m) feet:

the world's tallest ever tsunami wave, Lituya Bay, AK, 1958 (1.6 times as tall as the Eiffel Tower)

TSUNAMI MYTHS

In Japanese legends, a giant catfish called Namazu lives in the mud on the ocean floor, guarded by the god Kashima. If Kashima accidentally lets Namazu move, the fish thrashes around, causing earthquakes and tsunamis. Tsunami is a Japanese word meaning "harbor wave."

Towering waves

The Japanese artist Katsushika Hokusai (1760–1849) is famous for this print of a great wave with Mount Fuji in the background.

4 Approaching land
The waves slow down as they cross shallower coastal waters. They also grow taller—up to 30 times as high as in the open sea.

5 Reaching the shore
Before each wave breaks, the sea withdraws up to 0.5 miles (1 km). It then surges forward, creating a towering wall of water.

Wave energy
The waves' energy reaches from the surface all the way down to the seabed.

Coastal waves
Waves bunch together as the shallow seabed slows them down.

Withdrawing sea

Breaking wave

TSUNAMI PROTECTION

The 2004 Indian Ocean tsunami was so deadly because no warning system was in place. Since then, a DART warning system has been installed. Each DART station has an earthquake detector that sends signals to a floating buoy (left). Communications satellites pick up the signals and transmit warnings. This system is able to give several hours' warning before a tsunami arrives.

SPREADING INLAND

When tsunamis reach land, they behave differently from ordinary waves. Instead of breaking on the shore and withdrawing, tsunamis keep on coming. They surge inland, hour after hour, until their energy is used up and the water subsides.

TSUNAMI TIMELINE

On December 26, 2004, a magnitude 9.1 earthquake struck without warning in the rocks below the Indian Ocean. The earthquake triggered a series of devastating tsunamis.

SPREADING OUT

This map shows how the initial tsunami rippled outward around the earthquake's epicenter, and how long it took to spread across the Indian Ocean.

SOMALIA 6

MALDI 5

1. Swamped low-lying land
+15 minutes

Just 15 minutes after the ground stopped shaking, the first 33-foot (10-m) wave crashed onto the Aceh coast, in northern Sumatra, Indonesia. The waves flattened homes and killed around 130,000 people.

2. Tsunami hitting Phuket Beach
+2 hours

Within 2 hours, 16-foot (5-m) waves reached the beaches on the west coast of Thailand. Around 5,000 locals and tourists lost their lives. Some were carried out to sea and drowned. Others were crushed by the force of the water, or by debris carried in the waves.

3. Chennai Beach
+2 hours

In southeast India, the sea receded up to 0.5 miles (1 km) before the waves surged inland. Beach resorts and fishing villages vanished beneath the water, and nearly 10,000 people were killed.

FIRST WAVE

WAVES REACHED THAILAND

INDIA HIT

60 Troubled Water

WAVE HEIGHT

In the open ocean, the tsunamis were only 20 inches (50 cm) tall. As they entered shallow coastal waters, they grew until they were 16–33 feet (5–10 m) tall.

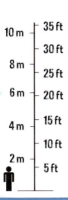

Patong Beach, Thailand
These photos show the beach before (left) and after (right) the tsunami struck.

INDIA ③
SRI LANKA ④
THAILAND ②
INDONESIA ①
EARTHQUAKE BEGAN

7:58 AM EARTHQUAKE BEGAN

Pent-up energy was suddenly released deep in the seabed. The earthquake, which shook the ground for 10 minutes, jolted trillions of tons of water directly above its epicenter, and caused a 1,000-mile-long (1,600-km-long) fracture along the seafloor.

SRI LANKAN TRAIN SWEPT AWAY

4 Twisted train tracks
+2 hours 30 minutes

Sri Lanka suffered 35,000 casualties as 20-foot (6-m) waves swamped its shores. On the island's southwest coast, the tsunami hit a crowded passenger train, killing 1,700 people. It was the country's worst ever train disaster.

MALDIVES SWAMPED

5 Wrecked boat, Kolhufushi Island
+4 hours

The flat, low-lying Maldives had almost no natural protection against the waves. The capital city was flooded, and around 80 people lost their lives.

WAVES HIT SOMALIA

6 Damage on the Cape of Hafun
+7 hours 30 minutes

After crossing 2,800 miles (4,500 km) of open ocean, the first tsunami reached the coast of Somalia, in Africa. Even though the waves had become weaker, they still washed away coastal villages, killing over 200 people and destroying boats and homes. To the south, the Kenyan coast was protected by coral reefs, and only one person drowned.

SUICHANG POWER PLANT, JIANGXI PROVINCE, CHINA

62 How People Cause Disasters

HOW PEOPLE CAUSE DISASTERS

FIND OUT

HOW do human activities cause disasters?
WHAT is global warming?
WHICH insect spreads a deadly disease?

CAUSING DISASTER

Every year, people cause disasters all around the world. These range from wildfires and marine pollution to global warming—potentially the biggest human-caused disaster of all time.

OUR TROUBLED WORLD

On today's crowded planet, human activities trigger disasters on a scale never seen before. We damage the natural environment on every continent, making survival harder for other living things. Some human-caused disasters strike suddenly, but many others build gradually, over months or years.

Wildfires

In some places, wildfires are part of nature's calendar. Problems arise when people live in areas prone to wildfires, such as in densely populated California. People may spark fires themselves, either by accident or deliberately.

Pollution

Pollution is the waste created when we manufacture things, use them, and throw them away. Major pollution disasters may occur by accident. In January 2022, an accident at an oil refinery in Peru leaked 6,000 barrels of crude oil into the sea and turned nearby beaches black.

LIVING IN DISASTER ZONES

Every year, there seem to be more natural disasters, partly because more of them make the news worldwide. However, our growing population also means that more people are living in danger zones. If a natural disaster such as a volcanic eruption or an earthquake strikes, more people are at risk.

Living near Mount Etna

People have lived on the slopes of Etna, an active volcano on the Italian island of Sicily, for thousands of years—drawn by its rich, fertile soil.

Deforestation

For thousands of years, people have cut down forests to clear land for farming. Today, this includes tropical forests, such as the Amazon. Deforestation prevents absorption of carbon dioxide, contributing to global warming.

2 BILLION:
the number of people affected worldwide by desertification

Environmental disasters
This rusty trawler sits on the dried-up bed of the Aral Sea—once a giant lake in Central Asia. Diverting water to irrigate crops has shrunk the lake by around 90 percent, killing its wildlife.

Desertification
In the Gansu province of China, overfarming has reduced supplies of underground water, causing the soil to dry out and reducing farmland to dusty desert. Desertification and drought can often lead to famine.

ASIA

Etna · Aral Sea · CHINA · BANGLADESH · AUSTRALASIA · INDONESIA

People have destroyed about one-fifth of Earth's coastal wetlands.

Mud volcanoes
This man is trying to rescue his belongings from his home, which was swamped by streams of thick, toxic mud. The mud oozed out of the ground when a team of engineers accidentally triggered a mud volcano at Sidoarjo, Indonesia, while drilling for natural gas. Around 30,000 people lost their homes.

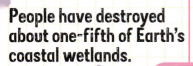

Coastal flooding
People cross streets via bamboo bridges in the flooded port of Narayanganj, in Bangladesh. Coastal flooding during storms has become more common along coasts where natural "shock absorbers," such as wetlands and mangrove forests, have been destroyed to build towns.

500 MILLION:
the number of people who live on or near active volcanoes

65

THIRSTY WORK

For these Turkana women in northern Kenya, a drought means a lot of extra work. To collect water, they have to climb down a deep well in a dry riverbed, using steps that have been dug by hand. Droughts are natural events, although unlike most disasters, they can last for many years. In places that normally have dry climates (such as northern Kenya), people are used to water shortages. However, prolonged droughts can lead to great hardship. The dry, dusty ground makes it impossible to raise cattle or grow crops, and the result can be famine—one of the biggest disasters of all.

GLOBAL WARMING

You can't always see it or feel it, but Earth's climate is changing. By burning fossil fuels, we are making our planet warmer—a change that could spell disaster for all living things.

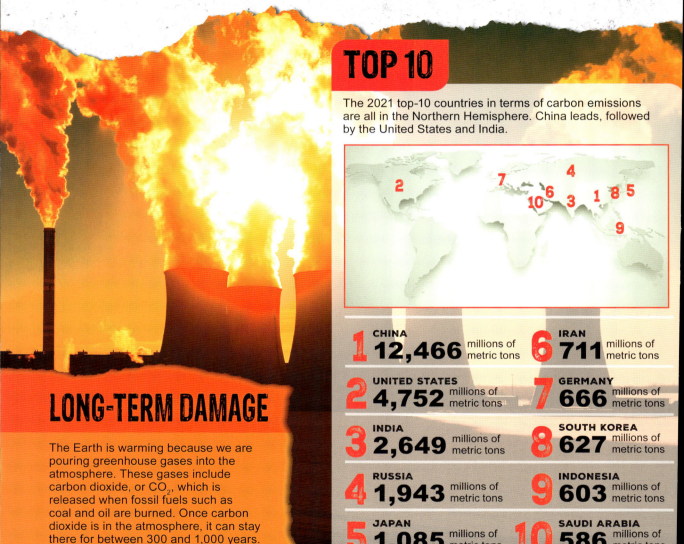

TOP 10

The 2021 top-10 countries in terms of carbon emissions are all in the Northern Hemisphere. China leads, followed by the United States and India.

1 CHINA — 12,466 millions of metric tons
2 UNITED STATES — 4,752 millions of metric tons
3 INDIA — 2,649 millions of metric tons
4 RUSSIA — 1,943 millions of metric tons
5 JAPAN — 1,085 millions of metric tons
6 IRAN — 711 millions of metric tons
7 GERMANY — 666 millions of metric tons
8 SOUTH KOREA — 627 millions of metric tons
9 INDONESIA — 603 millions of metric tons
10 SAUDI ARABIA — 586 millions of metric tons

LONG-TERM DAMAGE

The Earth is warming because we are pouring greenhouse gases into the atmosphere. These gases include carbon dioxide, or CO_2, which is released when fossil fuels such as coal and oil are burned. Once carbon dioxide is in the atmosphere, it can stay there for between 300 and 1,000 years.

POWER STATIONS

Our modern lifestyles demand more energy for our homes and factories. Power stations burn fossil fuels to generate electricity, releasing CO_2.

GREENHOUSE EFFECT

Earth is kept warm by the greenhouse effect, in which some of the Sun's heat is trapped by greenhouse gases. Without this natural feature of the atmosphere, parts of our planet would freeze. However, the effect is intensified because of the increase of greenhouse gases in the air.

How it works
Greenhouse gases trap heat from the Sun. The more gas there is, the warmer Earth becomes.

1. SUN'S ENERGY
Heat from the Sun reaches the Earth's atmosphere. Some is reflected, but most passes through to reach the ground.

2. HEAT FROM EARTH
The Earth's surface radiates heat back toward space.

3. TRAPPED HEAT
Some of the heat is trapped by greenhouse gases in the atmosphere.

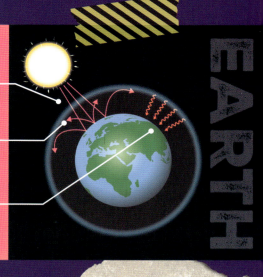

MORE EXTREME WEATHER

Rising average temperatures are associated with dramatic changes in weather patterns. Worldwide, the top-10 warmest years since records began all occurred since 2010. Extreme weather events are happening more often and are more intense. They can wreak havoc on people's communities and livelihoods.

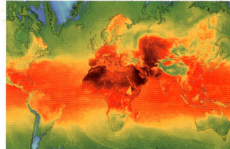

Heat waves
In July 2023, 83 million people were under a heat advisory. Heat waves are occurring three times more often than they did in the 1960s. Heat waves cause illness and death and damage crops.

Wildfires
Hotter and drier weather is a big factor in longer and more active fire seasons. The area of fire burned in the western United States doubled between 1984 and 2015.

Hurricanes
While they are not becoming more frequent, hurricanes in the United States are becoming more dangerous. Severe flooding and wind damage occur more often.

Flooding
Storms in recent years have been delivering higher rain totals. In July 2023, about 14 million people were affected by flooding in a "1-in-1,000-year weather event."

Drought
For the past two decades, the American West has experienced the most extreme mega-drought in 1,200 years, marked by receding reservoirs and water shortages.

FUTURE DISASTER

Imagine how you would feel if your home disappeared beneath ocean waves. That is the prospect facing some island nations as the world continues to warm. Sea level rise is just one of the effects of global warming. Other changes are also underway—and the warmer it gets, the more disastrous they will be.

DISAPPEARING WORLD

Even in the next few decades, rising sea levels may make low-lying islands across the world uninhabitable. Their land area will shrink, storm damage will increase, and there will be no fresh water.

WORLD EFFECTS

Scientists have been studying some of the disastrous effects of global warming since the 1980s—from its impacts on a small reef ecosystem to those on a whole continent. While some people doubt that global warming is taking place or that it is caused by humans, 97 percent of scientists agree that the evidence is now all around us.

Islands in danger

Micronesia, in the Pacific Ocean, has thousands of low-lying island nations. Kiribati, pictured, has over 30 islands, all of them less than 6.5 feet (2 m) above the high-tide mark.

Melting glaciers

Mountain glaciers and ice caps are melting and retreating worldwide. Their meltwater ends up in the oceans, contributing to sea level rise.

Dying reefs

Corals cannot survive in water that is too warm or contains too much dissolved CO_2. In the tropics, reefs are "bleaching" and dying off.

Extinction

Animals are at risk from climate change. Many species of some amphibians, for example, have already become extinct because of global warming and disease.

EYEWITNESS

NAME: Tapua Pasuna
DATE: 2019
LOCATION: Tuvalu archipelago
DETAILS: Tapua Pasuna, daughter of one of the country's lawmakers, describes the changes.

" I left in 2010 to go to university. When I came back I immediately noticed the difference. The heat is sometimes unbearable now, and the erosion is also dramatic. . . . I feel like this is a part of who I am and I shouldn't just run away from it, even though it is disappearing. To just abandon it at such a time as this. . . . I don't feel like I can do that. "

WHAT CAN YOU DO?

You have a carbon footprint—it is the amount of carbon dioxide your lifestyle releases into the atmosphere. Think about how you travel, how you use electricity, where your food comes from, what you wear, and the goods you buy. There are things that you can change in your everyday life that can make a difference.

1. Check your carbon footprint
Use an online carbon footprint calculator to figure out the things you are doing that release CO_2. Then you can decide how to reduce the amount you release.

2. Out and about
Walk or bike instead of traveling in a car to reduce greenhouse gas emissions and air pollution.

3. Around the house
Turn off lights and unplug electronic gadgets when they are not in use. They use power even when off.

4. Reduce and recycle
Carbon dioxide is released into the atmosphere by the factories that make the products we buy. Instead of buying new things, mend your clothes or fix things you already have.

5. Back to nature
Plant a tree or grow your own vegetables. Plants help to remove carbon dioxide from the air.

TACKLING GLOBAL WARMING

Global warming cannot be stopped, because it is already happening. But we can prevent a runaway disaster by changing how we live—from the way that we get energy to the things that we buy and use.

Wind turbines
A typical wind turbine can generate 6.5 million kilowatt-hours (kWh) of electricity a year—that's enough to power 1,500 homes.

RECYCLING

Recycling doesn't just get rid of garbage—it also reduces your carbon footprint. Making things from recycled materials takes much less energy than making them from raw materials. The percentage amounts of energy saved are shown below.

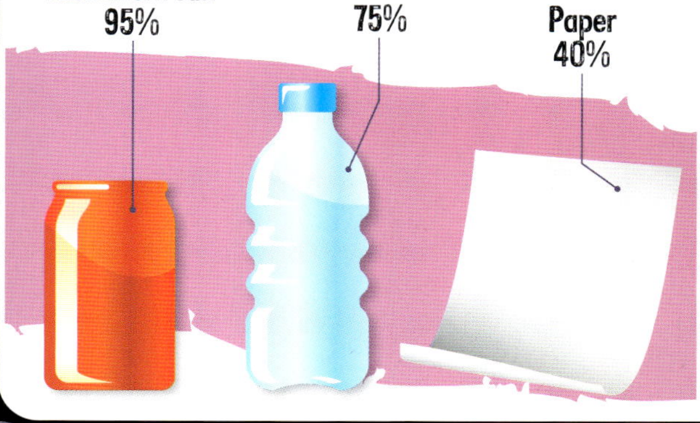

- Aluminum can **95%**
- Plastic water bottle **75%**
- Paper **40%**

CAR CARBON EMISSIONS: *

GAS-POWERED
87 lb CO_2 per 100 miles (24.53 kg CO_2 per 100 km)

HYBRID ELECTRIC
57 lb CO_2 per 100 miles (16.06 kg CO_2 per 100 km)

ALL-ELECTRIC
54 lb CO_2 per 100 miles (15.22 kg CO_2 per 100 km)

* Includes all emissions related to fuel production, processing, distribution, and use.

CARBON CAPTURE

Some countries employ emergency measures that help limit our CO_2 output. Carbon is captured before it escapes into the air and then stored inside rocks below the seabed.

1. CAPTURE
CO_2 is captured at power stations where fossil fuels are burned.

2. COLLECTION
Compressed CO_2 is pumped to natural gas drilling rigs at sea.

3. BURIAL
The gas is pumped into tiny holes in sandstone that once held natural gas.

4. STORAGE
The CO_2 can remain trapped inside for millions of years.

REDUCING GREENHOUSE GASES

Around the world, countries have set themselves goals for reducing CO_2 emissions. Five main goals are shown on this page. Two of them—recycling household waste and using renewable energy sources—are things that everyone can do.

1 Reforestation
Planting forests helps remove CO_2 from the atmosphere, because trees use and store carbon as they grow. It stays locked inside while the trees are alive.

2 Renewable energy
Nuclear power is a way of producing electricity without emitting carbon. However, it is controversial because of the risk of nuclear disaster.

3 Energy from waste
Nonrecyclable waste can be burned and used to generate electricity. This helps reduce fossil fuel consumption and also reduces the amount of dumped waste.

4 Farming
Biofuel crops such as maize or sugarcane can be used to power vehicles. They can take the place of fuels such as gas and diesel.

5 Smart meters
Electronic meters monitor and adjust energy use in factories, offices, and homes to keep it at a minimum.

73

OVERBURDENED EARTH

Seen from space at night, Earth is a sparkling web of light that shows the spread of people across its surface, especially in densely populated areas like cities. With 250 babies born each minute, our world's population is growing by about 70 million per year. Every one of us uses energy, which places increasing pressure on Earth's dwindling natural resources and contributes to global warming.

The United Nations called November 15, 2022,

8 BILLION DAY:
the day the world's population reached 8 billion.

PANDEMICS

Large or global outbreaks of infectious diseases have brought disaster to humankind throughout history. Pandemics, such as influenza (flu), cholera, and recently COVID-19, still break out, affecting millions of people.

800 BC
Early plagues
Plague originally meant any infectious disease that killed large numbers of people. Dating from 800–612 BC, this Assyrian amulet, or lucky charm, was meant to protect its owner from a plague.

1500s
Measles, smallpox, and mumps
In many places, diseases such as measles are endemic, or always present, and people develop a resistance to them. However, they were unknown in the Americas before the Europeans introduced them. The people of the Inca and Aztec empires had no resistance to the diseases, and over 10 million people died. The first vaccine for measles was developed in 1963.

AZTEC DRAWING OF VICTIM

---

800 BC —

430 BC — The Plague of Athens was probably an outbreak of typhoid fever, which raged for over four years in ancient Greece.

AD 165–180 — The Antonine Plague was either smallpox or measles. It killed 2,000 people a day in the city of Rome, with a final death toll of 5 million.

AD 541–750 — The Plague of Justinian was the first recorded outbreak of bubonic plague. It killed 25 million people in Europe before finally fading away.

1096 — Typhus emerged in Europe during the Crusades. Spread by lice, it is sometimes called camp fever.

MID-1300s —

1500s —

1580 — The first influenza pandemic was recorded in Europe. It had spread from Asia via Africa.

16...

MID-1300s
The Black Death
The Black Death was an outbreak of bubonic plague in Europe, starting in October 1346. Spread by fleas from rats, it caused painful swellings called buboes, which gave the disease its name. There was no known treatment, and infected families were often shut inside their homes.

ILLUSTRATION OF THE BLACK DEATH FROM THE TOGGENBURG BIBLE (1411)

1600s
Typhus
This killer disease thrives in crowded, unsanitary conditions. In Europe, the disease killed millions between the 17th and 20th centuries. The first typhus vaccine was developed in 1937.

Typhus killed a third of infected people in the 1600s.

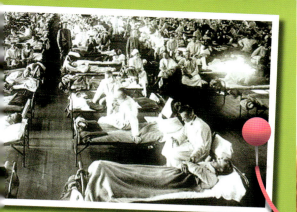

1764
Smallpox
In 1764, English doctor Edward Jenner successfully vaccinated a patient against smallpox—one of the world's deadliest diseases. In 1958, a worldwide vaccination program was launched, and the last natural case of smallpox was recorded in 1977.

1918
Spanish flu
Originating in the United States, this pandemic killed 50 million people worldwide in 1918–1919, more than the deaths caused by World War I. (Its nickname comes from wartime miscommunication.)

Spanish flu infected a quarter of the world's population.

VICTIMS IN A TEMPORARY HOSPITAL

2019
COVID-19
COVID-19 is a virus that affects people's breathing systems. The first cases emerged in Wuhan, China, in December 2019, and the virus spread quickly worldwide. The WHO declared COVID-19 a pandemic on March 11, 2020. Between 2020 and 2022, countries put lockdowns in place to slow the spread of the virus. The first vaccines were introduced in December 2020.

COVID-19 VACCINATION

Yellow fever struck Philadelphia, Pennsylvania, killing about 10 percent of the city's population.

1665 — 1764 — 1793 — 1816 — 1897 — 1918 — 1956–58 — 1981– — 2019

The Great Plague of London, an outbreak of bubonic plague, killed at least 100,000 people, emptying the city's streets.

The first vaccine against bubonic plague was developed.

Avian flu broke out in China, triggering a global pandemic and killing up to 4 million worldwide.

1816
Cholera
Cholera is easily spread by contaminated water and food. The first pandemic swept through southern Asia in 1816, causing hundreds of thousands of deaths. Six more pandemics followed. The first vaccine was developed in the late 19th century.

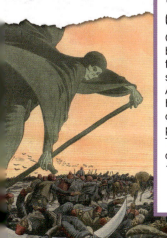

PAINTING OF DEATH BRINGING CHOLERA

1981 ONWARD
HIV/AIDS
First identified in the United States in 1981, the human immunodeficiency virus (HIV) has since spread worldwide. AIDS, the disease caused by HIV, has killed more than 35 million people. According to the World Health Organization (WHO), the African region is worst affected. About 390,000 people in this region died from HIV-related causes in 2023.

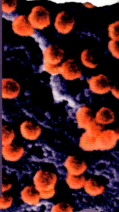

MAGNIFICATION OF AIDS VIRUS PARTICLES BUDDING ON A HUMAN LYMPH CELL

77

MALARIA

Malaria is a natural disaster—and a human one. For thousands of years, it has been one of the most deadly infectious diseases. Parasites transmitted by mosquitoes multiply in a person's liver and blood. This causes severe headaches, liver damage, and potentially fatal fevers.

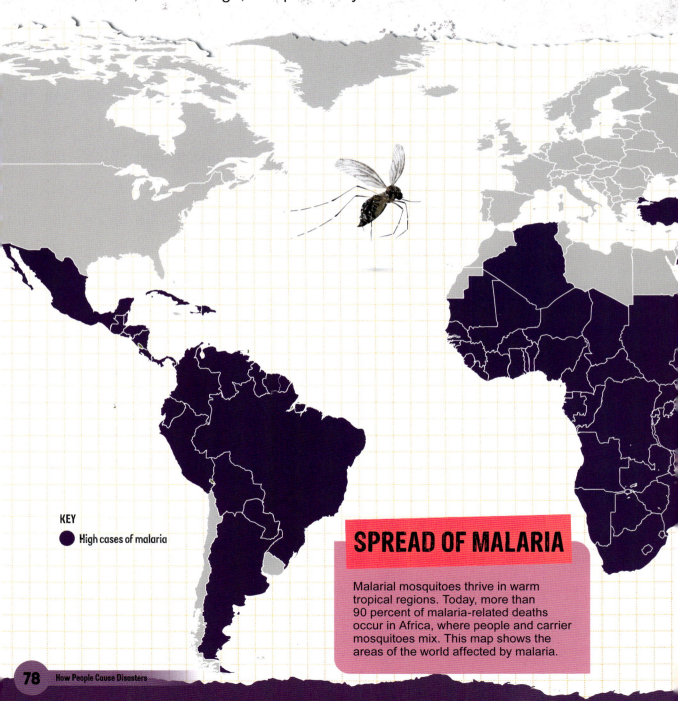

KEY
■ High cases of malaria

SPREAD OF MALARIA

Malarial mosquitoes thrive in warm tropical regions. Today, more than 90 percent of malaria-related deaths occur in Africa, where people and carrier mosquitoes mix. This map shows the areas of the world affected by malaria.

WORLDWIDE:

one child dies every minute from malaria.

PREVENTING MALARIA

Mosquitoes breed in stagnant water, so draining ponds and ditches makes it harder for them to survive. Using nets helps prevent bites, because the insects cannot fly through the fine mesh. If the nets are treated with insecticide, the mosquitoes die.

Expensive nets and vaccines

Drugs, insecticides, and even nets are too expensive for many in regions where malaria is endemic. The first malaria vaccine was recommended by the WHO in 2021, but money is desperately needed for further research on drugs and vaccines.

Tiny killer

Magnified over 100 times, a female anopheles mosquito gets ready for a meal of human blood. The amount it drinks is tiny, but as it feeds it can collect parasites that cause malaria. The mosquito can then spread the disease when it bites its next victims.

ASTEROID COLLIDING WITH PLANET EARTH

THE THREAT FROM SPACE

FIND OUT

WHEN will the Sun destroy our planet?
HOW do solar storms affect our daily lives?
WHAT killed the dinosaurs?

ASTEROID IMPACT

About 66 million years ago, a huge asteroid plunged through the atmosphere and smashed into Earth. The dinosaurs and many other animals were wiped out as fires raged and clouds of debris filled the air. It was a global disaster—and it could happen again.

Target Earth
Ever since Earth formed, it has been bombarded by rocks from space. Meteorites, or small rocks, fall to Earth without causing any damage. Asteroids are much bigger and much more dangerous. The one that killed off the dinosaurs was at least 6 miles (10 km) wide and weighed over 1 trillion tons.

Fatal impact
Traveling at 50 times the speed of sound, a 1-trillion-ton asteroid would have unimaginable destructive power. It could gouge out an impact crater 93 miles (150 km) wide, then instantly vaporize, blocking out light from the Sun. In the months of darkness that would follow, three-quarters of the world's plants would die.

Near-Earth objects
NASA constantly monitors near-Earth objects (NEOs) that speed past Earth on their orbits around the Sun. Most are not dangerous, but some come closer to Earth than our Moon does. If one was tugged off course by Earth's gravity, it could hit our planet, with devastating results.

LOCAL DEVASTATION
NEO'S SIZE: 82 ft (25 m) in diameter—the size of a house
SPEED: 31,000 mph (50,000 kph)
COULD DESTROY: An area up to 1.5 mi (2.5 km) wide

REGIONAL DEVASTATION
NEO'S SIZE: 164 ft (50 m) in diameter—as tall as a 15-story office building
SPEED: 31,000 mph (50,000 kph)
COULD DESTROY: A major city

EXTINCTION EVENT
NEO'S SIZE: 1 mi (1.5 km) in diameter—the length of 15 soccer fields
SPEED: 31,000 mph (50,000 kph)
COULD DESTROY: Most of life on Earth

CRATERS ON THE MOON

On Earth, impact craters from asteroids are worn away until few traces remain. But the Moon has no weather, so its craters are easy to see—clear evidence of the many impacts the Moon has experienced since it formed over 4 billion years ago.

Large and small
Many of the Moon's craters are smaller than a pinhead. The largest are over 185 miles (300 km) wide.

TUNGUSKA FIREBALL

In 1908, a mysterious fireball destroyed a huge expanse of forest around Tunguska, a remote village in central Siberia, Russia. The explosion was probably caused by a meteoroid or comet breaking up high above the ground.

Flattened forest
Signs of the Tunguska event were still visible nearly 20 years later, although the explosion left no crater.

EYEWITNESS

NAME: Unknown
DATE: June 30, 1908
LOCATION: 19 miles (30 km) from the Tunguska River, in Russia
DETAILS: Interviewed by a scientific expedition, a reindeer herder described what he saw and heard during the Tunguska event.

> The ground shook and incredibly prolonged roaring was heard. Everything round about was shrouded in smoke and fog from burning, falling trees. Eventually the noise died away and the wind dropped, but the forest went on burning.

SOLAR STORMS

Asteroids are not the only hazard that threatens us from space. The Sun—our nearest star—seethes with energy, which sometimes erupts in colossal solar storms. An extra-large storm can knock out electric systems on Earth, bringing normal life to a halt.

IN THE LINE OF FIRE

As energy and matter stream outward from the Sun, they create huge disturbances in space, affecting all of the planets that they pass. Earth is one of the inner planets, so it feels the full impact. Farther out in the solar system, the effect of solar storms dwindles. When the Sun is quiet, flares occur less than once a week, but at the height of a storm, they can occur every day. Giant flares can be longer than the distance between Earth and the Moon.

How a solar flare works

As a solar flare bursts through the corona, or the outer layer of the Sun's atmosphere, it often forces out clouds of charged particles. This coronal mass ejection (CME) produces solar energetic particles (SEPs). They can cause disturbances in Earth's magnetic field.

CME
A coronal mass ejection (CME) is produced as the flare streams into space.

Sun's magnetic field

Sunspots
Pairs of sunspots are often connected by curved solar prominences.

Solar flare
A flare erupts from an area of intense magnetic activity.

SEPs
A CME produces solar energetic particles (SEPs).

The Threat from Space

THE SOLAR MAXIMUM

The Sun has a strong magnetic field that builds up to a stormy maximum every 9–14 years, with maximums in 2000 and 2014. During a solar maximum, planet-size sunspots track across the surface of the Sun, while loop-shaped prominences arch into space. Energy and matter are ejected in solar flares. The most recent solar maximum happened at the end of 2024.

A FUTURE SOLAR STORM COULD KNOCK OUT ELECTRICITY WORLDWIDE.

Shock wave
A mass of SEPs produces a shock wave.

Earth

SEPs in space
SEPs stream through space in straight lines.

Shaped by the Sun
Earth's magnetic field forms a "tail" as SEPs stream past.

Wave at Earth
A wave of SEPs causes geomagnetic storms on Earth.

AURORAS

Auroras are lights that appear in the sky, usually at high latitudes near Earth's magnetic poles. They are created when charged particles from the Sun collide with atoms high up in Earth's atmosphere. Auroras are brightest during solar storms, when there is increased activity on the Sun's surface.

Northern lights
Sometimes called the northern lights, auroras are usually bluish green and appear to hang in the sky like curtains.

THE 1859 SOLAR STORM

In August 1859, the largest solar storm ever reported was seen on the Sun's surface. It featured giant sunspots and solar flares. Within hours, Earth's magnetic field was disrupted, and the first effects were felt around the world. Telegraph systems failed, and brilliantly colored auroras shimmered in the skies as far south as Cuba, Hawaii, and Rome in Italy.

Effects on Earth
A repeat of the 1859 solar storm would have serious effects on Earth, since we now rely so heavily on electric power. Power grids could be disrupted, as well as anything electronic, including global positioning systems (GPS) and vital hospital equipment. A solar storm could affect the Internet by disabling electronics and cutting off power.

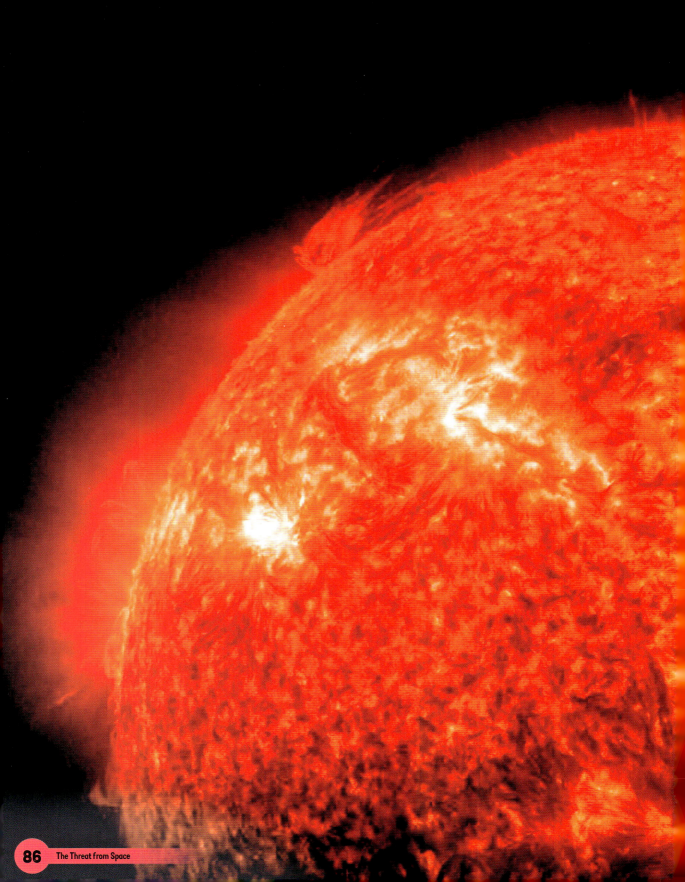

THE FINAL DISASTER

Almost all life on Earth depends on heat and light from the Sun. However, like all stars, the Sun will change as it ages. In about 5 billion years, as it starts to run out of fuel, it will begin to swell, until it eventually engulfs our planet and wipes out all traces of past life.

GLOSSARY

aa lava Thick, sticky lava that has a rough surface when it solidifies.

aftershock A small tremor that happens after a bigger earthquake. Aftershocks are dangerous because they can cause already damaged buildings to collapse.

asteroid A large piece of rock that orbits (travels around) the Sun.

biofuel A fuel made from plants. Biofuel crops include sunflowers, sugarcane, and corn, as well as many other plants that produce oils rich in energy.

carbon dioxide A colorless gas found in the atmosphere, absorbed by plants when they grow. It plays an important role in the greenhouse effect.

carbon footprint The amount of carbon-containing gas emitted by things that a certain person or entity uses (such as lights, computers, or cars) and actions that it takes (such as manufacturing goods).

cinder cone A volcano with a wide, steep crater composed of small pieces of lava.

comet A piece of rock and ice that orbits the Sun. Unlike asteroids, comets often have long tails of dust and gas.

condensation funnel A funnel inside a tornado, formed by droplets of water.

conduit A vertical tunnel in a volcano that allows magma to flow upward into a volcano's vent.

convergent boundary A type of boundary in Earth's crust where neighboring plates collide head-on.

coral bleaching An effect on corals that results from the warming of the sea. The corals turn white because they expel the colorful algae that normally live inside them.

core The innermost region of Earth, composed mainly of iron. This creates Earth's magnetic field.

cornice An overhanging slab of snow on top of a mountain ridge. Cornices have sharp edges that point away from the wind.

corona The outermost layer of the Sun, which stretches far into space. The corona is composed of charged particles and has a temperature of over 1,800,000°F (1,000,000°C).

crust The rocky outer layer of Earth, whether under the sea or exposed as dry land.

DART A tsunami warning system that uses surface buoys and seismometers on the seabed. The seismometers detect seabed earthquakes, and the buoys pass the signals to satellites. DART stands for Deep-Ocean Assessment and Reporting of Tsunamis.

deforestation Destruction of forests for their timber or to clear land for farms.

divergent boundary A type of boundary in Earth's crust where two plates pull apart.

doldrums At sea, a zone of light winds that stretches around the Equator.

endemic Present in a given place or region.

epicenter The point on Earth's surface directly above the hypocenter of an earthquake.

evaporate To change from a liquid to a vapor (gas).

extinction The permanent disappearance of a species of animal or plant after the last of the species has died out.

eye The clear, calm zone at the center of a hurricane.

fault A crack in Earth's crust where chunks of rock slip past one another. Faults vary hugely in size—some are small, but others are thousands of miles long.

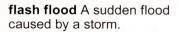

flash flood A sudden flood caused by a storm.

fossil fuel A fuel that is formed from the ancient remains of living things. Fossil fuels include coal, oil, and natural gas. They contain high levels of carbon, and they release carbon dioxide when they are burned.

geologist A scientist who studies Earth.

global warming A change in Earth's climate that causes the planet to warm up. Global warming has happened many times in the past and is happening now.

greenhouse effect The trapping of heat by gases in a planet's atmosphere. The greenhouse effect keeps Earth warm by making the planet absorb energy that would otherwise escape into space.

greenhouse gas Any gas in the atmosphere that is part of the greenhouse effect. The most important greenhouse gases are carbon dioxide and water vapor.

humid Full of water vapor.

hypocenter The site below the ground where an earthquake starts.

hypothermia A dangerous drop in body temperature, which can lead to disorientation and death.

inundate To completely cover with water.

lahar A flow of mud or debris, usually triggered by a volcanic eruption.

lava Magma, or molten rock, that has erupted onto Earth's surface.

lava field A plain of solidified lava, left behind after volcanic eruptions. Some plains cover hundreds of square miles.

magma Hot, molten rock in Earth's mantle, below the crust. Magma reaches the surface through volcanoes and volcanic vents.

mantle The layer of Earth between the crust and core.

meteor The visible trace of a meteoroid passing through the atmosphere. Meteors are sometimes called shooting stars.

meteorite A meteoroid that reaches Earth's surface instead of burning up in the atmosphere.

meteoroid A small particle of debris or rock traveling through space.

midocean ridge A submerged mountain range in the middle of an ocean where volcanic activity forms new seabed.

monsoon A wind that changes direction with the seasons. It is derived from the Arabic word *mausim*, meaning "season."

monsoon climate A tropical climate with two different seasons—one wet and one dry. The monsoon wind brings heavy rain during the wet season.

mudslide A river of waterlogged mud that rushes downhill in a torrent. Mudslides often occur on slopes after prolonged heavy rain.

normal fault A crack in Earth's crust where two neighboring plates slowly diverge, or pull apart.

pahoehoe lava Lava that flows easily and that has a glassy skin when it cools.

pandemic An outbreak of disease that infects many people at the same time.

parasite An organism that lives inside or on another living thing, using it for food. Small animals can be parasites, as can tiny microorganisms that cannot be seen with the naked eye.

plate One of the huge pieces of rock that make up Earth's crust, or outer layer. Plates are slowly moving, usually about 0.5 in (1.3 cm) each year.

plug The hard tower of solid lava that is sometimes left when the rest of a volcano is eroded, or worn away, by the wind and rain.

pollution Anything that contaminates the natural world and harms living things. Pollutants include gases that escape into the air, and chemicals that find their way into water and soil.

pumice A light volcanic rock formed from frothy lava. Some kinds of pumice are so light that they can float.

reforestation Replanting of forests that have been cut down. Reforestation helps counteract global warming, because trees absorb carbon dioxide from the air.

renewable energy Energy from natural sources that are continuously renewed. It includes energy from the Sun, wind, and moving water, as well as geothermal energy from the ground.

saturate To completely soak with water, so that no more can be absorbed.

seismologist A geologist who studies earthquakes, their causes, and their effects.

seismometer An instrument that records vibrations produced by earthquakes. By using seismometers at different locations around the world, scientists can pinpoint an earthquake's epicenter.

shield volcano A volcano that is shaped like a huge, gently sloping dome. Shield volcanoes are formed from runny lava that spreads easily when it erupts.

soil creep The slow downhill movement of soil. Creep often happens in wet conditions, or when soil freezes and then thaws.

solar flare A sudden eruption of hydrogen gas in the Sun's atmosphere, caused by changes in the Sun's magnetic field.

solar maximum A peak in the buildup of the Sun's magnetic storms, which occurs every 9–14 years.

solar prominence A huge, loop-shaped band of glowing gas that stretches outward from the surface of the Sun.

storm surge A rise in sea level caused when a hurricane or a typhoon drifts over land.

stratovolcano A volcano that is built up from many layers of lava and ash.

strike-slip fault A crack in the Earth's crust where two neighboring plates slide horizontally past each other.

sunspot A relatively cool patch on the surface of the Sun that appears dark in comparison to its bright surroundings. Sunspots are areas of intense activity on the Sun's surface, caused by the Sun's magnetic field.

supercell A rotating thunderstorm that can produce tornadoes.

thrust fault A crack in Earth's crust where two neighboring plates converge, or come together. As the plates collide, one is thrust below the other.

Tornado Alley An area in the US Midwest, stretching from Texas to Nebraska and Iowa, that experiences more tornadoes than any other area in the world.

transform boundary A type of boundary in Earth's crust at which two neighboring plates slide past one another.

tremor A shaking or vibrating movement of the earth.

tropical cyclone A powerful tropical storm that often forms over the sea. Tropical cyclones include hurricanes, which form over the Atlantic Ocean from May to November, and typhoons, which form over the northwest Pacific Ocean from June to November.

tropical depression A low-pressure weather system with heavy rain and clouds. Tropical depressions have maximum wind speeds of 39 mph (63 kph).

tropical storm A storm that starts in the tropics. Tropical storms have maximum windspeeds of 74 mph (119 kph).

tropics The region between the Tropic of Cancer (23.5 degrees north of the Equator) and the Tropic of Capricorn (23.5 degrees south of the Equator). A tropical climate has high temperatures and heavy rain for at least part of the year.

tuned mass damper A heavy weight mounted in skyscrapers and other buildings to protect them during an earthquake.

twister A tornado.

vent In a volcano, an opening that lets magma escape to the surface of the Earth.

volcanologist A geologist who studies volcanoes, including how they are formed and how they erupt.

90 Glossary

INDEX

A
aa lava 48
Afghanistan
  avalanches 26
  blizzards 24, 25
Africa
  disease 76, 77, 78, 79
  droughts 66
  flooding 8, 55, 56
  landslides 55
  lightning 22, 23
  monsoons 56
  mudslides 33
  tsunamis 61
  wildfires 23
aftershocks 41, 42, 43
AIDS 77
air
  greenhouse gases 68, 69, 71
  pressure 12, 16, 19
  weather systems 10, 11, 56
airplanes 29, 47
Alabama
  tornadoes 17
Alaska
  avalanches 27
  tsunamis 59
Aleppo, Syria 39
Amazon Rainforest 64
animals
  extinction 70
Antakya, Turkey 39
Aral Sea 65
ash
  volcanic 46, 47, 48, 50, 51
Ashgabat, Turkmenistan 39
Asia
  monsoons 54, 55, 56, 57
  pandemics 76, 77, 78
asteroid impacts 80, 81, 82–83
Atlantic Ocean
  Mid-Atlantic Ridge 34, 35
atmosphere
  Earth 10, 11, 68, 69, 82
  greenhouse effect 69
  lightning 22–23
  Sun 84
aurora 11, 85
Australia
  flooding 55
  wildfires 28, 29
Australian banksia 28
avalanches 26–27
  avalanche packs 27

B
Bangladesh
  flooding 9, 65
  tornadoes 16, 17
barriers against avalanches 27
bicycles
  carbon footprint 71
blizzards 24–25
body temperature 25
bombs
  volcanic 46, 48
Brazil
  flooding 54
  landslides 8, 33
breaking waves 59
buildings
  earthquake protection 44
  wildfires 28
buoys 58, 59

C
California 54, 64
Canada
  blizzards 24, 25
  tornadoes 16
  wildfires 9
car travel
  reducing 71
carbon dioxide
  carbon capture 73
  increase 68
  reduction 71
carbon emissions 68, 72
carbon footprint 71, 72
Casey, Sean 14
category 1 hurricanes 18, 20
category 3 hurricanes 19, 20,
category 5 hurricanes 18, 19, 20
category 5 storms 21
Cherrapunji, India
  rainfall 57
Chicago, IL
  wildfires 28
children
  earthquakes 45
  hurricanes 21
Chile
  earthquakes 38, 39
  volcanic eruptions 35
China
  avian flu 77
  carbon emissions 68
  desertification 65
  earthquakes 39, 44
  extreme cold 9
  flooding 55, 57
  monsoons 57
  wildfires 29
Christchurch, New Zealand
  earthquakes 38
cinder cones 50
climate
  warming 68–69, 70, 72, 74
clouds
  hurricanes 18–19
  lightning 22–23
  tornadoes 12–13
  weather systems 10–11, 26, 27
coastal flooding 65
cold conditions 9, 24–25
Colombia
  volcanic eruption in, 51
computers
  earthquake studies 36
condensation funnels 12, 13
conduits 46, 47
cones
  volcanic 46, 47, 50
convergent boundaries 35, 38
coral reefs 61, 70
cornice avalanches 26
coronal mass ejections (CMEs) 84
creep
  soil 32
creep meters 36
cyclones
  tropical 9, 18, 19

D
Damghan, Iran 39
dams 8, 43, 55
DART warning systems 58, 59
deadly earthquakes 8, 9, 39, 41, 42
deadly volcanoes 9, 51
deadly wildfires 8, 9, 28, 29
Death Valley, California, 54
debris slides 33
deforestation 64
Denali National Park 27
depressions
  tropical 18, 19, 20, 21
desertification 65
diseases 63, 76–77, 78–79
divergent boundaries 34, 35, 38
dogs 42
doldrums 11
dormant volcanoes 50
droughts
  human-caused 29, 69
  Kenya 66

E
Earth
  crust movement and formation 34–35, 36, 38
  heat from 71
  plate boundary 34–35, 36, 38, 42, 58
  population 64, 74–75
  satellite images 10, 18, 20, 21
  Sun's effect 10, 56, 71, 84, 86, 87
  temperature rises 70, 71
  unstable 30–31
earthquakes
  aftermath 42–43, 52
  building design 44
  causes 35, 38
  Chile 38, 39
  China 39
  deaths 39
  detectors 44, 59
  drills 45
  epicenter 38, 39, 58, 60, 61
  Haiti 39
  hypocenter 38, 58
  Indonesia 39, 60, 61
  Iran 39
  Italy 39, 47
  Japan 39, 45, 52
  landslides 34
  New Zealand 34, 38
  people at risk 36, 38, 42, 43
  Philippines 45
  prediction 44
  search and rescue 42, 43
  study of 36
  survivors 42
  Syria 9, 38, 39, 41, 42, 43
  tsunamis 38, 39, 44, 52, 60, 61
  Turkey 9, 30, 38, 39, 41, 42, 43
  Turkmenistan 39
  types of 38–39
  under the seafloor 58
earth scientists 36–37
electricity 68, 71, 72, 73
  in solar storm 85
energy
  production 72
  renewable 73
  of Sun 10, 71, 85, 87
Enhanced Fujita (EF) scale 16
equator
  lightning 22
  thunderstorms 11
erosion
  asteroid craters 82, 83
  climate change 71
  volcanoes 47
Etna, Mount 37, 64
exosphere 11
explosives
  blasting 27
extinction 70, 82
extinct volcanoes 46, 50
extreme weather
  global warming 64, 65, 70–71, 72, 74–75
  study of 72
eye of storm 19

F
famines 51, 65, 66
fault lines 34, 35, 36, 38, 42
firefighters 29, 43
fire, see wildfires
flooding 54–55
  Australia 55
  Bangladesh 9, 65
  Brazil 8, 54
  China 55, 57
  coastal 65
  flash floods 8, 54
  Pakistan 9, 54, 55, 57
  Portugal 54
  protection 55
  thunderstorms 11
  United States 54
Florida
  hurricanes 20
  tornadoes 17
Foraker, Mount
  avalanches 27
forests
  destruction 28, 29, 49, 64, 65, 83
  reforestation 73
  tropical 64
  wildfires 28–29, 64, 69
fossil fuels 68, 73
freezing conditions 24–25, 42
frostbite 24
fuel use 68, 73
funnels
  tornadoes 12, 13, 16
future disasters 37, 49, 70–71, 82

G
Galunggung volcano 51
gases
  greenhouse 68, 69, 71, 73
  greenhouse effect 69
  volcanic eruptions 37, 46, 47, 50
Geodimeters 36
geologists 36
Germany
  carbon emissions 68
geysers
  Yellowstone Park 35
glaciers 70
Glens Falls, NY
  avalanches 27
global lightning 22
global positioning systems (GPS) 85
global warming 63, 64, 68–69, 70, 72–73, 74
  deforestation 64
  effects 70, 71
  tackling 72–73
Greece
  plague of Athens 76
  wildfires 29
greenhouse gases 68, 69, 71, 73
Gulf of Mexico
  hurricanes 19, 20

H
hailstones
  giant 13
Haiti
  earthquakes 39

health
  HIV/AIDS 77
  malaria 78–79
  measles 76
  pandemics 76–77
  typhoid fever 76
  typhus 76
  vaccines 76, 77, 79
  yellow fever 77
heat waves 69
Herculaneum 47
Hokusai, Katsushika 59
hot spots 22, 35
Huang He River 55
human-caused disasters 64–65
hurricanes 18–19
  aftermath 20, 21
  inside 18, 19
  Katrina 18, 19, 20–21
  life of 18, 19
  measuring 18
  survivor stories 21
hypocenters 38, 58
hypothermia 24, 25

I
ice 10, 24–25, 48, 70
ice caps
  melting 70
Iceland
  volcanic eruptions 34, 51
icicles 25
ignition 28
India
  carbon emissions 68
  floods 9
  monsoons 57
  tsunamis 60
Indian Ocean
  cyclones 9
  tsunamis 59, 60–61
Indonesia
  earthquakes 39
  tsunamis 60, 61
  volcanic eruptions 9, 39, 50, 51
influenzas 76
insects
  disease 63, 78, 79
Internet
  effects of solar storm 85
Iran
  blizzards 24, 25
  carbon emissions 68
  earthquakes 39
islands
  sea level rise 70
Italy
  earthquakes 39
  volcanic eruptions 47, 51
  volcanoes 47, 51

J
Japan
  carbon emissions 68
  earthquakes 39, 45
  tsunamis 52, 53, 59
  volcanic eruptions 51
Jenner, Edward 77
jet streams
  polar 10
Joplin, MO,
  tornadoes 12, 13

L
LaGrange, WY 14
Lahaina, Maui
  wildfires 29
lahars 48–49
landslides
  Brazil 8, 54
  causes and effects 32–33
  due to thunderstorms 11
Laki volcano 51
lasers
  earthquake monitoring 36
lava
  Hawaii 49
  stratovolcanoes 46
  study of 37
  temperature 47
  types 48
lava bombs 48
levees 21
lightning
  strike survivors 23
  types 22
  wildfires 23, 28
Lisbon, Portugal 54
Lituya Bay, AK
  tsunami waves 59
London, UK 77
loose snow
  avalanches 26, 27
loudest noise 50
Louisiana Superdome 21
low air pressure 16, 19

M
magma 34, 35, 46, 47
magnetic fields 84, 85
Maldives
  tsunamis 61
Mars
  Olympus Mons 51
Martinique
  volcanic eruptions 51
Mauna Kea volcano 51
Mauna Loa volcano 51
maximum-strength hurricanes 19
Measeck, Ian 27
Merapi, Mount
  eruptions 9
mesosphere 11
Messina, Italy 39
meteorite 82
meteors 11
Mexico
  hurricanes 8
  volcanic eruptions 50
Micronesia 70
Mid-Atlantic Ridge 34, 35
midlatitude storms 11
Missouri
  tornadoes 12, 13, 17
monsoons 56–57
  China 57
  Nepal 57
  Pakistan 55, 57
Mont Pelée volcano 51
Moon
  craters 83
mosquitoes 78–79

motor vehicles 72, 73
Mount Etna volcano, Sicily 37, 65
Mount Foraker base camp 27
Mount Fuji 59
mud volcanoes 65
mudflows 33, 48
mudslides 32–33, 54

N
Nagin, Ray 20
Namazu (legendary catfish) 59
National Hurricane Center 20
National Weather Service 20
natural disasters, 2023 8–9
near-Earth objects (NEOs) 82
Nebraska
  tornadoes 17
Nepal
  earthquakes 39
  floods 9
  monsoons 57
Nevado del Ruiz volcano 51
New Orleans, LA
  hurricanes 18, 20–21
New York
  avalanches 27
  blizzards 24, 25
New Zealand
  earthquakes 34, 35, 38
  normal faults 38
North America
  blizzards 24, 25
northern lights 85
nuclear power 73

O
oil spills 64
Ojos del Salado volcano 51
Oklahoma City, OK
  tornadoes 17
Olympus Mons 51
oxygen 28

P Q
Pacific Ocean
  Ring of Fire 35
  sea level rise 70
pahoehoe lava 31, 48
Pakistan
  flooding 4,9, 54, 55, 57
  rockfalls 32
Palu, Indonesia 39
pandemics 76–77
Parícutin, Mount 50
Parkfield, CA
  earthquake study 36
Pasuna, Tapua 71
Patong Beach
  tsunamis 61
Pelée, Mont
  eruptions 51
pendulums 44

people and objects
  blown away 16
Philippines
  earthquakes 45
pillow lava 48
plagues 76, 77
planes 29
plants 28, 47, 71, 73, 82
Pliny the Younger 47
polar jet stream 10
poles
  auroras 85
pollution 64, 71
Pompeii 47
population growth 64, 74–75
Port-au-Prince, Haiti 39
Portugal
  flooding 54
power grids 85
power stations 68, 73
pressure drop 16
pumice 47

R
radars
  studying lava flow 37
  studying storms 14
radio
  avalanche rescues 27
rain
  freezing 24
  global warming 69
  mudslides 32, 33
  weather machine 10, 11
  see also flooding, monsoons
rain bands 19
rainfall
  highest 55, 57
recycling 72, 73
red sprites 22
reducing consumption 73
Reed, Jim 20
reefs
  dying 70
reforestation 73
renewable energy 72, 73
ridge of water 58
Ring of Fire 34, 35, 45
rivers
  flooding 54–55, 56, 57
rockfalls
  Pakistan 32
Russia
  blizzards 25
  carbon emissions 68
  icicles 25
  Tunguska fireball 83
  wildfires 29

S
Saffir-Simpson scale 18
San Andreas Fault 35, 36
satellites
  Earth's movement 36
  image of Earth 10–11

weather 10, 11, 18, 20, 21
  tsunamis 59
Saudi Arabia
  carbon emissions 68
seabed
  destruction 35
  detectors 59
  earthquakes 39, 58, 59, 61
  formation and seabed shifts 58
  seismometers 44
sea level rise 70
seismic waves 38, 39
seismographs 36, 39
seismologists 36
seismometers 44
sheet lightning 22
shield volcanoes 50, 51
Siberia
  Tunguska fireball 83
Sicily 37, 64
Sierra Leone 33
skiers 27
slab avalanches 26
sleet 24
slumping 32
smallpox 76, 77
smoke jumpers 29
snow
  avalanches 26–27
  cornice 26
  fracture zone 26
  polar jet stream 10
snowboarders 27
soil creep 32
solar energetic particles (SEPs) 84, 85
solar flares 84, 85
solar storms 84–85
Somalia
  tsunamis 60, 61
South Africa
  flooding 55
  lightning strikes 23
  wildfires 23
South America
  disease 78
South Korea
  carbon emissions 68
southern Europe
  flooding 55
Soviet Union see Russia
space
  asteroid impacts 82–83
  solar storms 84–85
  Sun's demise 86–87
Spanish flu 77
spiraling winds 10, 13, 19
Sri Lanka
  tsunamis 61
stepped leader stroke 23
storm chasers 14–15
"Storm of the Century" 25
storm surges 18, 19
storms
  global warming 69
  midlatitude 11
  solar 84–85
  tropical 18, 19, 20, 21

92 Index

storms and blizzards 24–25
  in weather front 10
strainmeters 36
strata 46
stratosphere 11
stratovolcanoes 46–47, 50, 51
strike-slip faults 38, 42
suction effect 19
Sullivan, Roy 23
Sumatra, Indonesia 39, 60
summer monsoons 55, 56, 57
Sun
  energy 10, 71, 84, 85
  demise of 86–87
  greenhouse effect 69
  solar storms 84–85
sunspots 84, 85
supercell storms 12, 13, 14, 17
survival pack 27
Suter, Matt 16
Syria, earthquake 9, 38, 39, 41, 42–43

T

Tabriz, Iran 39
Taipei, Taiwan
  earthquake protection 44
Tambora, Mount
  eruptions 51
Tangshan, China 39
telegraph equipment 85
temperature rise 69
Tennessee
  hurricanes 21
Texas
  blizzards 25
  flooding 54
  tornadoes 17

Thailand
  tsunamis 60, 61
thermosphere 11
Three Gorges Dam 55
thrust faults 38
thunderstorms 11, 12–13, 17, 18, 22
  see also lightning
Tornado Alley 17
Tornado Intercept Vehicle (TIV-2) 14–15
tornadoes 12–13, 14–15, 16–17
  aftermath 12
  formation 12–13, 16
  inside 12–13, 14–15
  life of 12–13
  scale 16
  statistics 16–17
  storm chasers 14–15
  studying 14–15
  warning signs 13
trapped heat 69
transform boundaries 34, 35, 38
travel
  carbon footprint 71
trees
  deforestation 64
  reforestation 73
tremors 36, 38, 44, 50
Tri-State Tornado 17
tropical cyclones 9, 18, 19
tropical depressions 18, 19, 20, 21
tropical forests 64
tropical storms 18, 19, 20, 21
troposphere 11
tsunamis 38, 39, 44, 52, 58–59, 60, 61
  in art 59
  forming 58–59

myths 59
  timeline 60–61
  warnings and protection 58, 59
  world's tallest 59
Tufenk, Steven 23
tumbling snow 27
Tunguska fireball 83
Turkey
  earthquakes 9, 30, 38, 39, 41, 42–43
Turkmenistan
  earthquakes 39
Tuvalu archipelago 71
twisters see tornadoes
typhoons
  formation 18–19

U

underground shelters 13
United Nations 43, 75
United States
  blizzards 24, 25
  carbon emissions 68
  faults and hot spots 35
  flooding 54
  hurricanes 18, 19, 20–21, 69
  ice storms 24, 25
  mudslides 33
  pandemics 77
  storm study 14–15
  tornadoes 12, 13, 16, 17
  tsunamis 59
  wildfires 9, 28, 29, 69
  Yellowstone Park geyser 35
Unzen, Mount
  eruptions 51
upper atmospheric lightning 22

V

vegetables
  growing own 71

vents (volcanoes) 46, 47
Vesuvius, Mount 47, 51
Victoria, Australia 29, 55
volcanic eruptions
  ash 46, 47, 48, 50, 51
  causes 34–35
  Chile 35
  Colombia 51
  Hawaii 49
  Iceland 34, 51
  Indonesia 9, 50, 51, 65
  Italy 47, 51, 64
  Japan 51
  Mexico 50
  mud 65
  people at risk 64
  statistics 50–51
  stratovolcanoes 46–47, 50
  types of volcano 50–51
volcanic plugs 47
volcanoes
  deaths 9, 37, 51
  dormant 50
  eruptions 9, 34, 35, 37, 46–47, 48–49, 50, 51, 64
  extinct 46, 50
  facts 50–51
  fallout 47
  life cycle 46–47
  plug 47
volcanologists 37
VORTEX2 project 14

W X

warnings
  avalanches 27
  earthquakes 38, 44
  flooding 55
  hurricanes 20
  tornadoes 13, 14
  tsunamis 58, 59
waste

reduction and reuse 72, 73
water
  human-caused problems 65
  in weather system 18, 19
water droplets
  electrically charged 22
wave energy 59
wave height 61
waves
  giant 58–59, 60–61
weather
  asteroid impact effects 82–83
  front 11
  machine 10–11
wildfires 28–29
  Australia 28, 29
  Canada 9
  China 29
  Greece 29
  human-caused 28, 64
  lightning strikes 23
  Soviet Union 29
  United States 8, 28, 29, 64
wind
  blizzards 24–25
  hurricanes 7, 8, 18–19, 20–21
  monsoons 53, 54, 55, 56–57
  tornadoes 7, 12–13, 14–15, 16–17
  turbines 72
  wildfires 28–29
winter monsoons 56
world blizzards 24–25

Y Z

Yangtze River 55, 57
Yellowstone Park
  geyser 35

CREDITS

Cover picture credits: All photos courtesy of **Shutterstock**.
Internal picture credits: All photos courtesy of **Shutterstock**, unless noted as follows: **Abestrobi/Wikimedia Commons:** 22bl (upper atmospheric lightning); **AFP/Stringer:** 61t (before and after the 2004 tsunami at Patong Beach, Thailand); **Alexander Joss/Wikimedia Commons:** 27ml (snow blasting); **Alexis Rosenfeld/Photo Researchers:** 28–29t (Canadair CL-215); **Alex Pedan/Shutterstock:** 24–25 (blizzard in New York, United States); **Alex Yeung/Shutterstock:** 73br (smart meter); **Alfred Wegener Institute for Polar and Marine Research/Wikimedia Commons:** 44mr (modern seismometer); **Alvinku/Shutterstock:** 44bc (101 pendulum); **amdadphoto/Shutterstock:** 9mr (floods in Chattogram, Bangladesh); **Anton Herrington/Shutterstock:** 55mr (flooding, South Africa); **AP Tolang/Shutterstock:** 57br (flooding in Kathmandu, Nepal); **Army Air Corps Photo 40400AC, copy provided by Dr. Robin Rose:** 29mc (smoke jumper); **Asianet-Pakistan/Shutterstock:** 55tr (flooding, Pakistan); **Associated Press:** 11br (landslides near Caracas, Venezuela), 21tl (people seeking shelter in the Louisiana Superdome), 23br (Roy Sullivan), 29 (fire truck at Black Saturday wildfire, Australia), 54ml (flooding, Nigeria), 54bl (flooding, Brazil); 64–65b (smoking Mount Etna), 65mr (desertification, China); **Beth Swanson/**

Shutterstock: 70bc (dying reefs); **BJ Warnick/Alamy Stock Photo:** 21bl (satellite image of New Orleans flooding); **Bruce Omori/Paradise Helicopters/EPA-EFE/Shutterstock:** 48–49 (lava flow); **Caitlin Mirra/Shutterstock:** 21tc (flood in New Orleans, United States); **Cire notrevo/Shutterstock:** 10bc (Hurricane Beryl in Texas, United States); **David A. Hardy, www.astroart.org:** 82–83 (asteroid colliding with Earth); **David Parker/Science Photo Library:** 36mc (strain meters at Parkfield in California, United States); **David Rydevik/Wikimedia Commons:** 60bc (tsunami hitting beach in Phuket, Thailand); **Doga Ayberk Demir/Shutterstock:** 9mr (earthquake destruction in İskenderun, Turkey); **Doug Lemke/Shutterstock:** 70br (rare frog); **Dr. Cecil H. Fox/Photo Researchers, Inc:** 77br (magnification of AIDS virus); **Drimi/Shutterstock:** 73bl (energy from waste); **dyl0807/Shutterstock:** 57tr (aftermath of monsoon, China); **easyshoot/Shutterstock:** 28ml (hot, windy weather); **Eye of Science/Photo Researchers, Inc:** 79bl (magnified female mosquito); **FabioConcetta/Dreamstime.com:** 39bc (Haiti earthquake, 2010); **Fæ/Wikimedia Commons:** 76tl (amulet to ward off plague); **Fletcher & Baylis/Science Source:** 28mr (charred seed cone); **Focus Pix/Shutterstock:** 33tr (mudslide in Rio de Janeiro, Brazil); **Gary Hincks/Science Source:** 32bc (soil creep), 32br (slumping), 33bl (debris slide), 33bc (mudflow), 33br (rockfall), 47m (ash, lapilli, and bombs), 56 (winter and summer monsoons); **gopixgo/Shutterstock:** 65tr (drought in the Aral Sea, Asia); **Handout/Getty Images:** 21tr (coast guard helicopter rescuing child); **HannaTor/Shutterstock:** 69br (drought in Arizona, United States); **Harley Kingston/Shutterstock:** 55br (flooding, Australia); **Harper/Shutterstock:** 25ml (icicles); **Hedayatullah Amid/EPA/Shutterstock:** 26ml (avalanche in Panjshir, Afghanistan); **Henryk Kotowski/GFDL/Wikimedia Commons:** 60br (tsunami in Chennai, India); **Ikluft/Wikimedia Commons:** 36l (San Andreas Fault in the Carrizo Plain in California, United States); **Inayat Ali (Shimshal):** 2, 32–33 (rockfall in Pakistan); **iStockphoto:** 22ml (cloud to ground lightning), 22mc (cloud to cloud lightning), 27mc (snow barriers), 28bl (wildfire type of land), 35br (Yellowstone geyser, United States), 39br (seismograph), 73mc (reforestation), 73bc (farming vehicle); **Jaden Schaul/Shutterstock:** 64tl (wildfire in California, United States); **Janne Hämäläinen/Shutterstock:** 64bl (Amazon River); **Jasminko Ibrakovic/Shutterstock:** 42br (search and rescue, Turkey); **Jeremy Bishop/Photo Researchers, Inc:** 37bl (basalt lava rock); **Jeremy Horner/Alamy Stock Photo:** 61bc (tsunami damage, Maldives); **Jezper/Shutterstock:** 68tr (world map); **JIMIN LAI/Staff:** 61bl (destroyed train tracks, Sri Lanka); **Jim Reed/Science Source:** 13br (giant hailstones in Kansas, United States), 20tr (man in Hurricane Katrina); **J. Scott Applewhite/AP Photo:** 10bl (weather front); **Katrina's Kids Project:** 21br (drawings by Denisha); **Lee Prince/Shutterstock:** 70bl (melting glacier); **Library Book Collection/Alamy Stock Photo:** 61br (tsunami damage in Somalia, Africa); **Linda Johnsonbaugh/Dreamstime.com:** 20br (evacuation route sign); **LukeTDB/iStock:** 6–7, 22ml (lightning above city); **Make Believe Ideas:** 34–35 (world map), 35tr (transform boundaries), 35mr (divergent boundaries), 35mr (convergent boundaries), 38ml (normal fault), 38mc (thrust fault), 38bl (strike-slip fault), 50tl (stratovolcano), 50ml (cinder cone), 50ml (shield volcano), 50tr (active volcano), 50mr (dormant volcano), 50mr (extinct volcano); **Malcolm Teasdale:** 38r (twisted rail tracks); **Matt Hage/Alamy Stock Photo:** 27 (avalanche at Mount Foraker in Alaska, United States); **Michael Duff/Getty Images:** 33tc (mudslide in Freetown, Sierra Leone); **Mike Hollingshead/Science Source:** 12mc, 12mr, 13ml, 13mc, 13mr (tornado in Nebraska, United States); **MPAK/Alamy Stock Photo:** 52–53 (aftermath of earthquake and tsunami in Sendai, Japan); **NASA:** 10–11 (Earth from space), 22tr (lightning around Earth), 74–75 (Earth at night), 83tl (crater on the moon), 84–85 (solar storm illustration), 86–87 (the Sun); **NASA/Science Photo Library:** 18bc, 18br, 19bl, 19bc, 19br (satellite image of Hurricane Katrina); **NOAA:** 20tl (tropical depression), 24mr (workers trying to free a locomotive trapped in snow in New York, United States); **NOAA/NGDC:** 58br (DART warning system); **NOAA/Wikimedia Commons:** 20bl (satellite image of Hurricane Katrina); **NOEL CELIS/Stringer:** 44–45 (earthquake drill in Manila, Philippines); **Nicoletta25/Shutterstock:** 9br (wildfire smoke in New York, United States); **NigelSpiers/Shutterstock:** 34bc (earthquake damage in Kaikoura, New Zealand); **NurPhoto/Getty:** 39mc (Turkey/Syria earthquake, 2023); **Olexa/Shutterstock:** 28ml (fuel supply); **OAR/National Undersea Research Program (NURP)/Wikimedia Commons:** 48bl (pillow lava); **Oleg Senkov/Shutterstock:** 69mc (heatwave map); **PA Images/Alamy Stock Photo:** 11bc (upturned aircraft following hurricane); **Patrick Landmann/Photo Researchers:** 47tc (plaster cast of victim); **PRILL Mediendesign und Fotografie/Shutterstock:** 55tl (Three Gorges Dam on the Yangtze River, China); **punksid/Shutterstock:** 44l (Taipei 101 tower); **Rumman Production/Shutterstock:** 30–31 (earthquake damage in Hatay, Turkey); **Ryan McGinnis/Alamy Stock Photo:** 12–13bc (tornado damage in Missouri, United States), 14bl and 14–15 (Tornado Intercept Vehicle 2); **Sawaya Photography/Getty Images:** 33tl (mudslide in Washington, United States); **Science Source/Photo Researchers:** 83tr (flattened forest in Tunguska, Russia); **Sigit Pamungkas:** 65mr (man in mud volcano, Indonesia); **Sk Hasan Ali/Shutterstock:** 9tr (cyclone in Cox's Bazar, Bangladesh), 65br (flooding, Bangladesh); **Stephen & Donna O'Meara/Photo Researchers:** 48ml (pahoehoe lava); **Stephen Morrison/EPA/Shutterstock:** 66–67 (drought, Kenya); **Tatonka/Shutterstock:** 73mr (nuclear power station); **Tim Loughhead/Precision Illustration:** 13tl (supercell storm); 13tr (condensation funnel), 18–19 (hurricane formation), 22–23b (how electric charge builds); 26tr (loose snow avalanche), 26mr (slab avalanche), 26br (cornice avalanche), 46bl (birth of stratovolcano), 46r (active stratovolcano), 47bl (stratovolcano erosion), 47br (volcanic plug), 55bl (river flooding), 58–59 (how a tsunami forms); **Tolga Ildun/Shutterstock:** 43b (tent city for survivors, Turkey); **Trevor Bexon/Shutterstock:** 69mr (wildfire in California, United States); **Twintyre/Shutterstock:** 43t (earthquake damage, Turkey); **USGS:** 36mc (creep meter in California, United States), 47mc (ash particle); **USGS/J. D. Griggs:** 48mc (scientists documenting lava flow speed), 48mb (lava bomb); **US Air Force photo by Senior Airman Joshua Strang/Wikimedia Commons:** 85bl (aurora above Alaska, United States); **US Army Photographer/Wikimedia Commons:** 77tl (Spanish Flu ward in Kansas, United States); **US Navy photo by Photographer's Mate 2nd Class Philip A. McDaniel:** 39mc (Indonesia earthquake, 2004); **US Navy photo by Photographer's Mate Airman Patrick M. Bonafede:** 60bl (tsunami in Sumatra, Indonesia); **WHO:** 78–79 (spread of malaria map); **Wikimedia Commons:** 59mr (Hokusai's *The Great Wave of Kanagawa*), 76tr (Aztec drawing), 76bc (image from Toggenburg Bible), 77bl (painting of death bringing cholera); **Yuyang/Dreamstime.com:** 44mc (ancient detector); **ZUMA Press, Inc./Alamy Stock Photo:** 39tc (Chile earthquake, 1960).